Graffiques!

By Adrienne Kleinschmidt

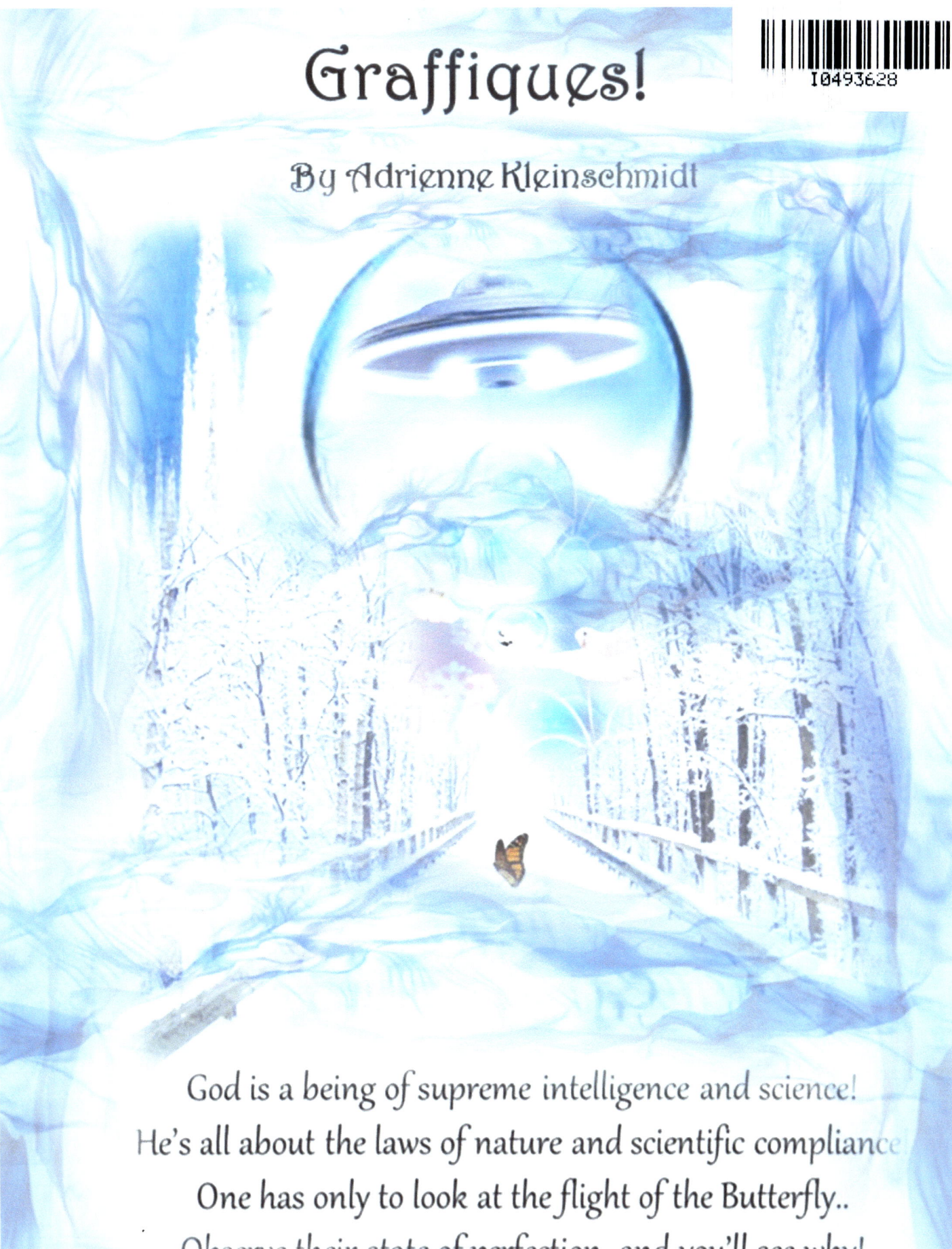

God is a being of supreme intelligence and science!
He's all about the laws of nature and scientific compliance
One has only to look at the flight of the Butterfly..
Observe their state of perfection, and you'll see why!

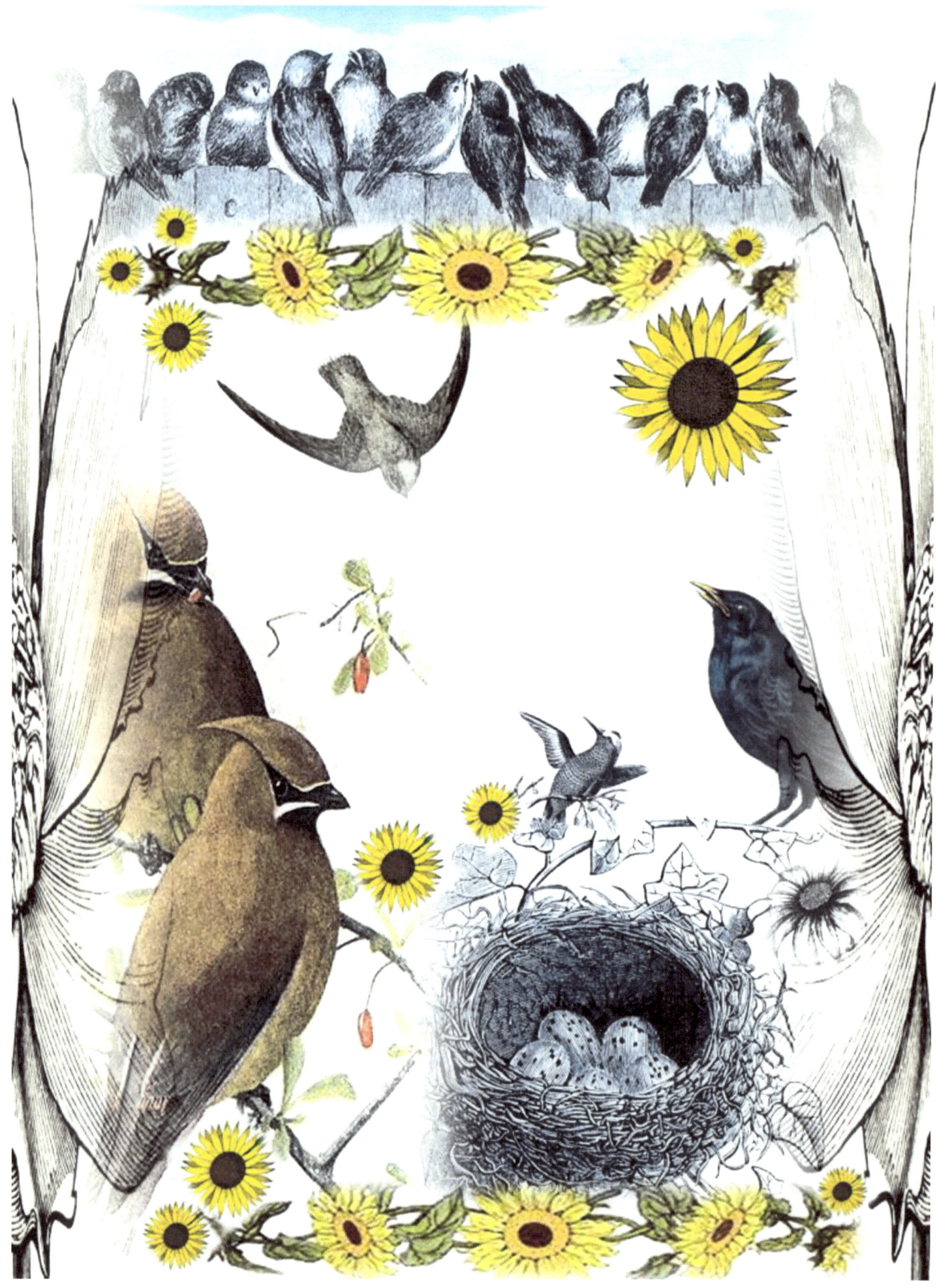

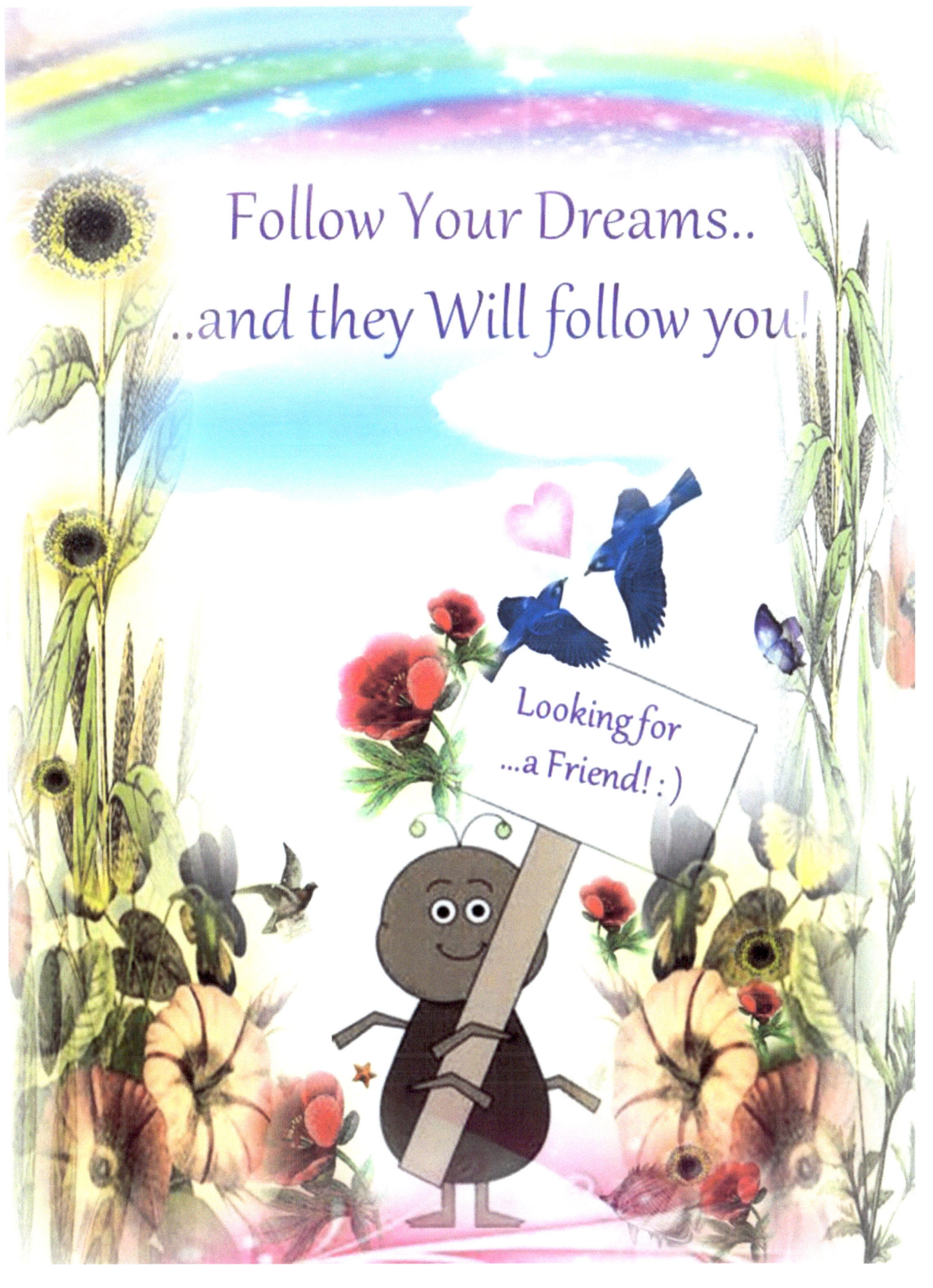

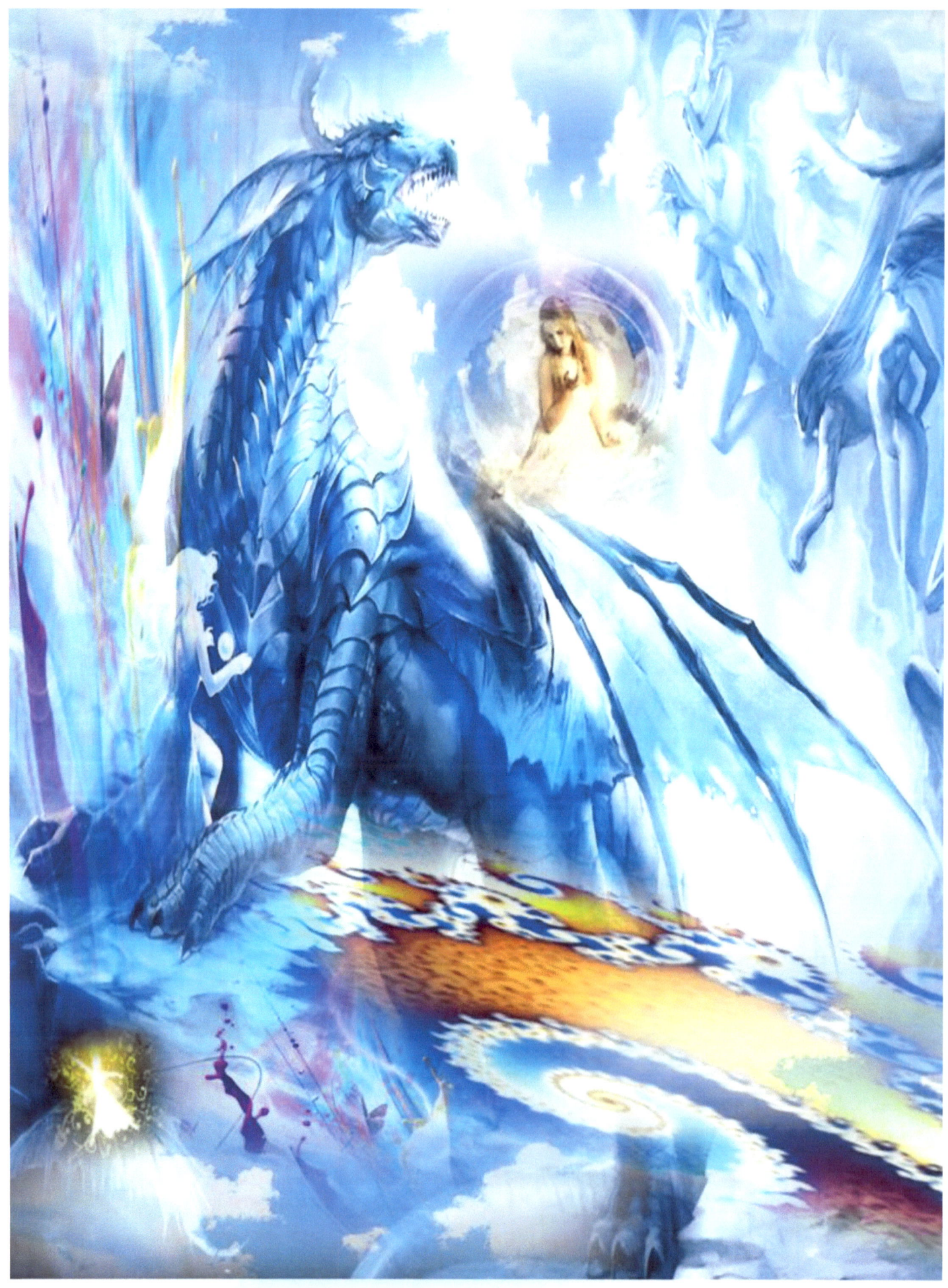

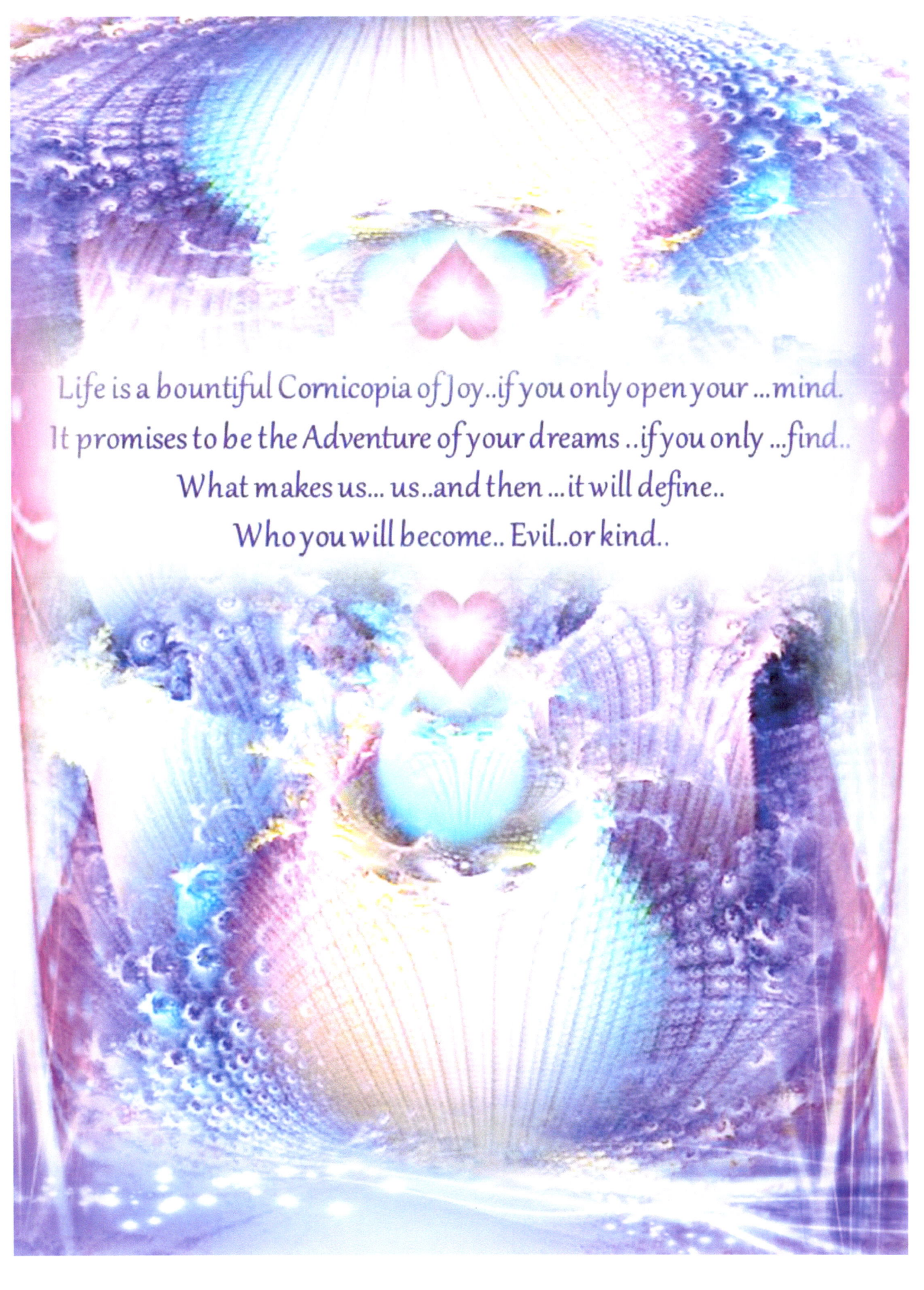

Life is a bountiful Cornicopia of Joy..if you only open your ...mind.
It promises to be the Adventure of your dreams ..if you only ...find..
What makes us... us..and then ...it will define..
Who you will become.. Evil..or kind..

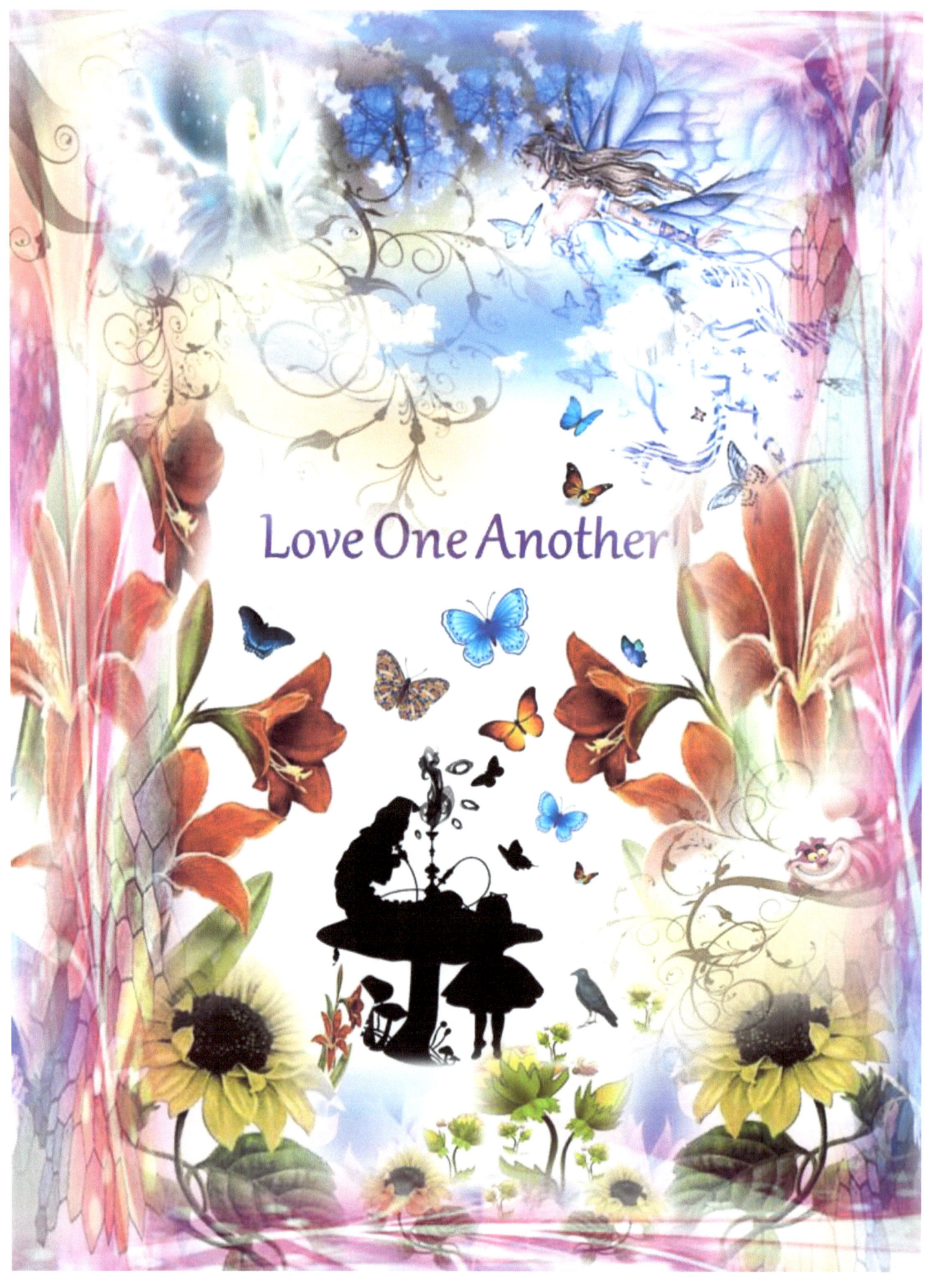

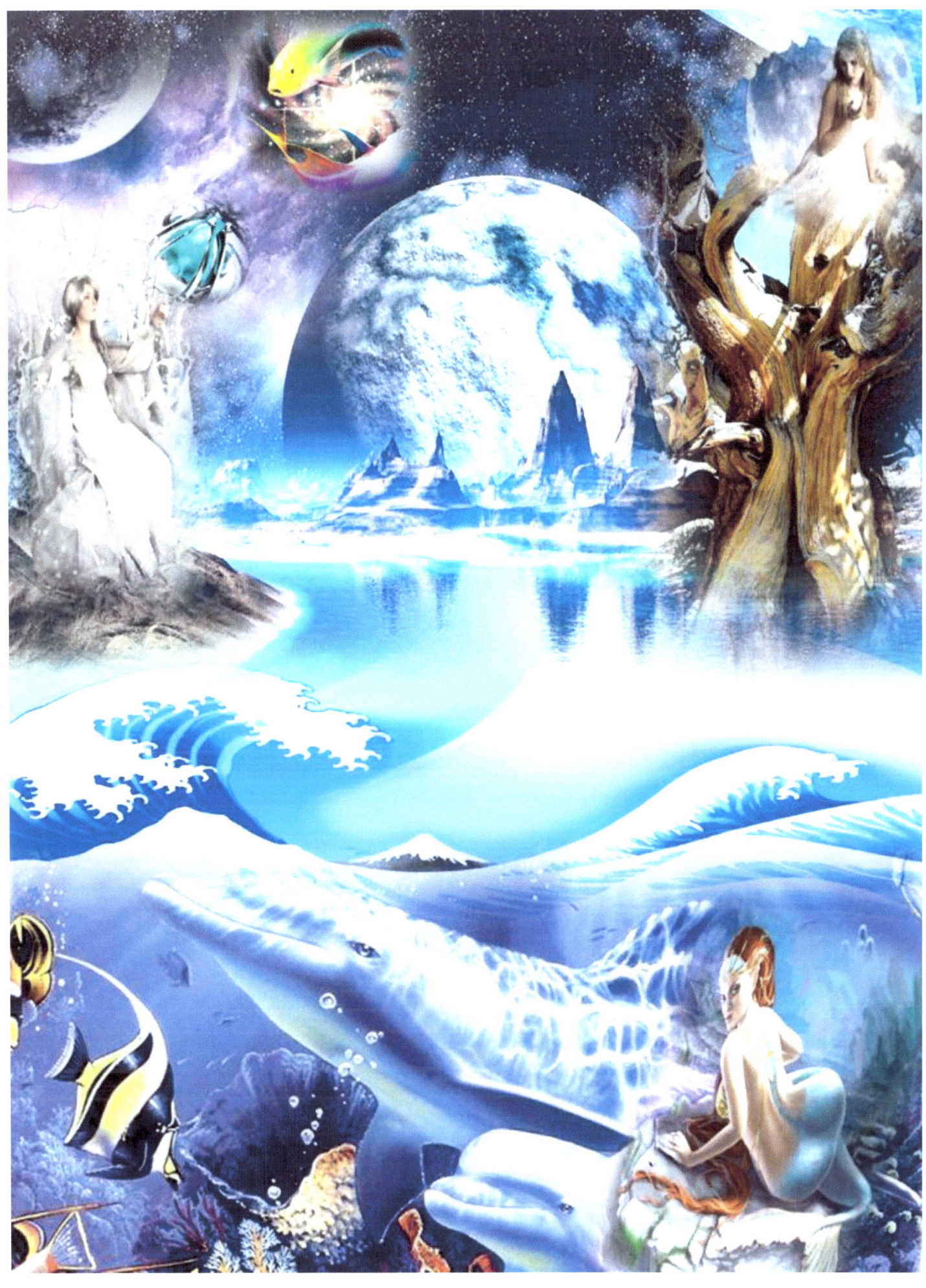

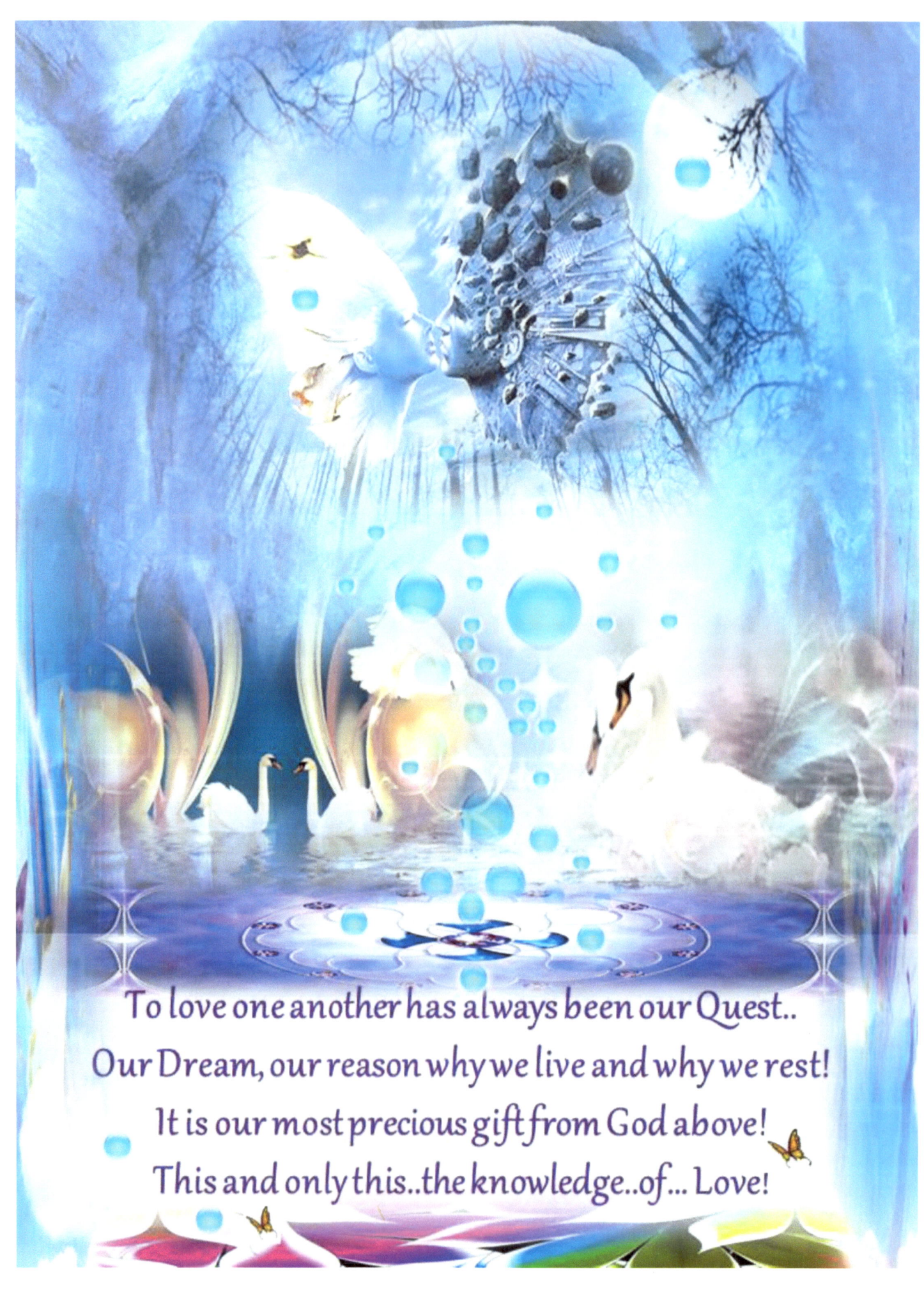

To love one another has always been our Quest..
Our Dream, our reason why we live and why we rest!
It is our most precious gift from God above!
This and only this..the knowledge..of... Love!

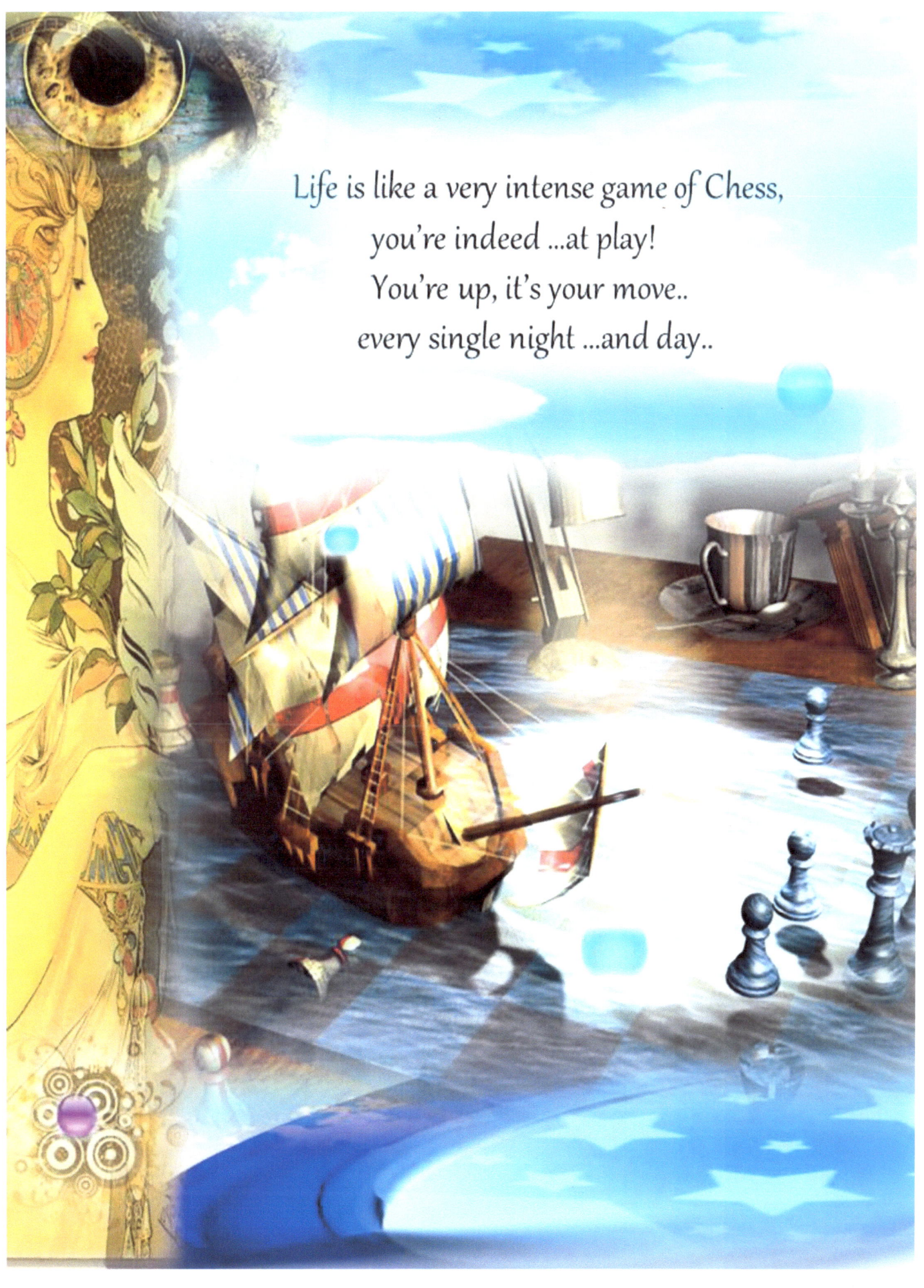

Life is like a very intense game of Chess,
you're indeed ...at play!
You're up, it's your move..
every single night ...and day..

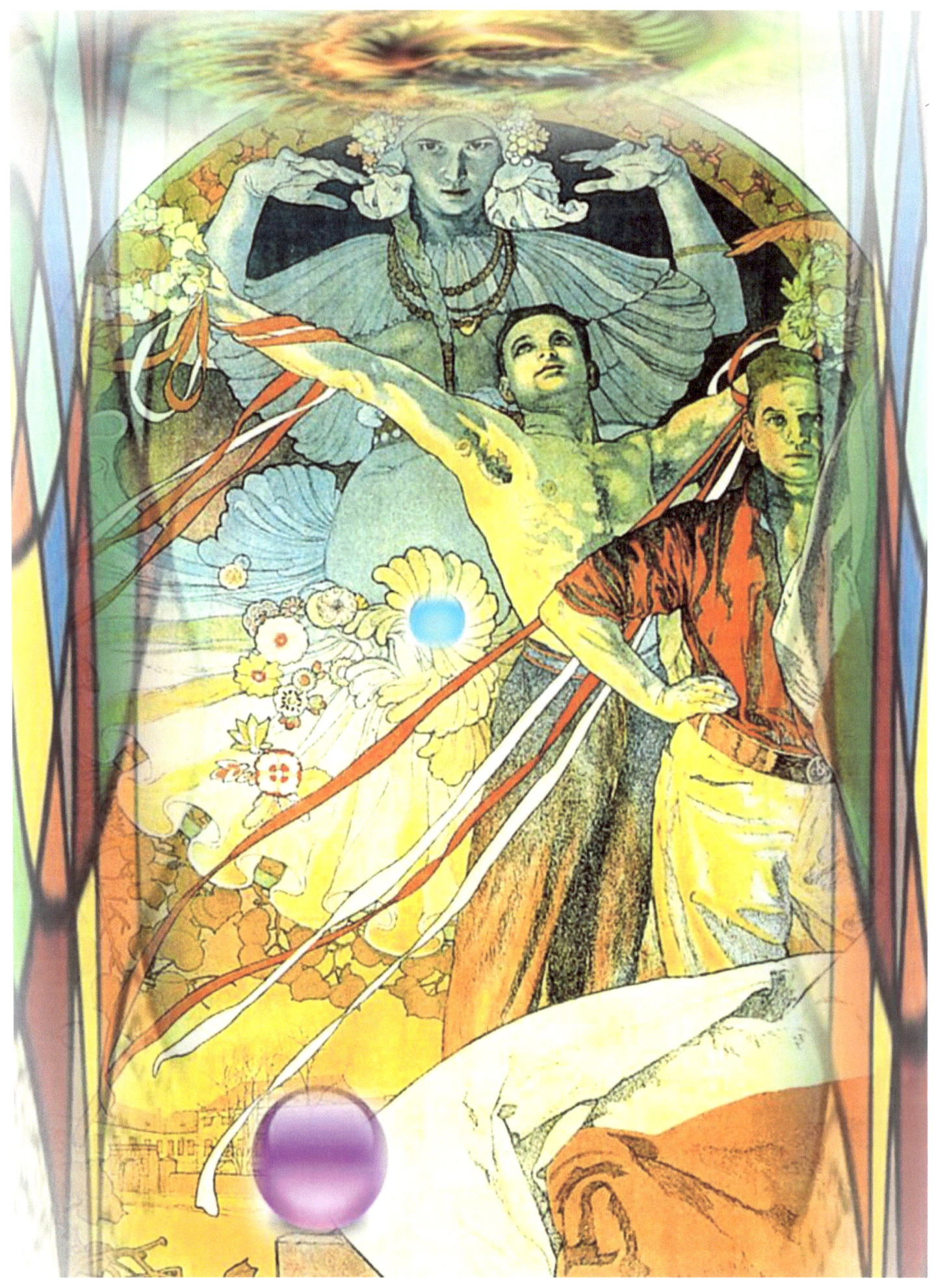

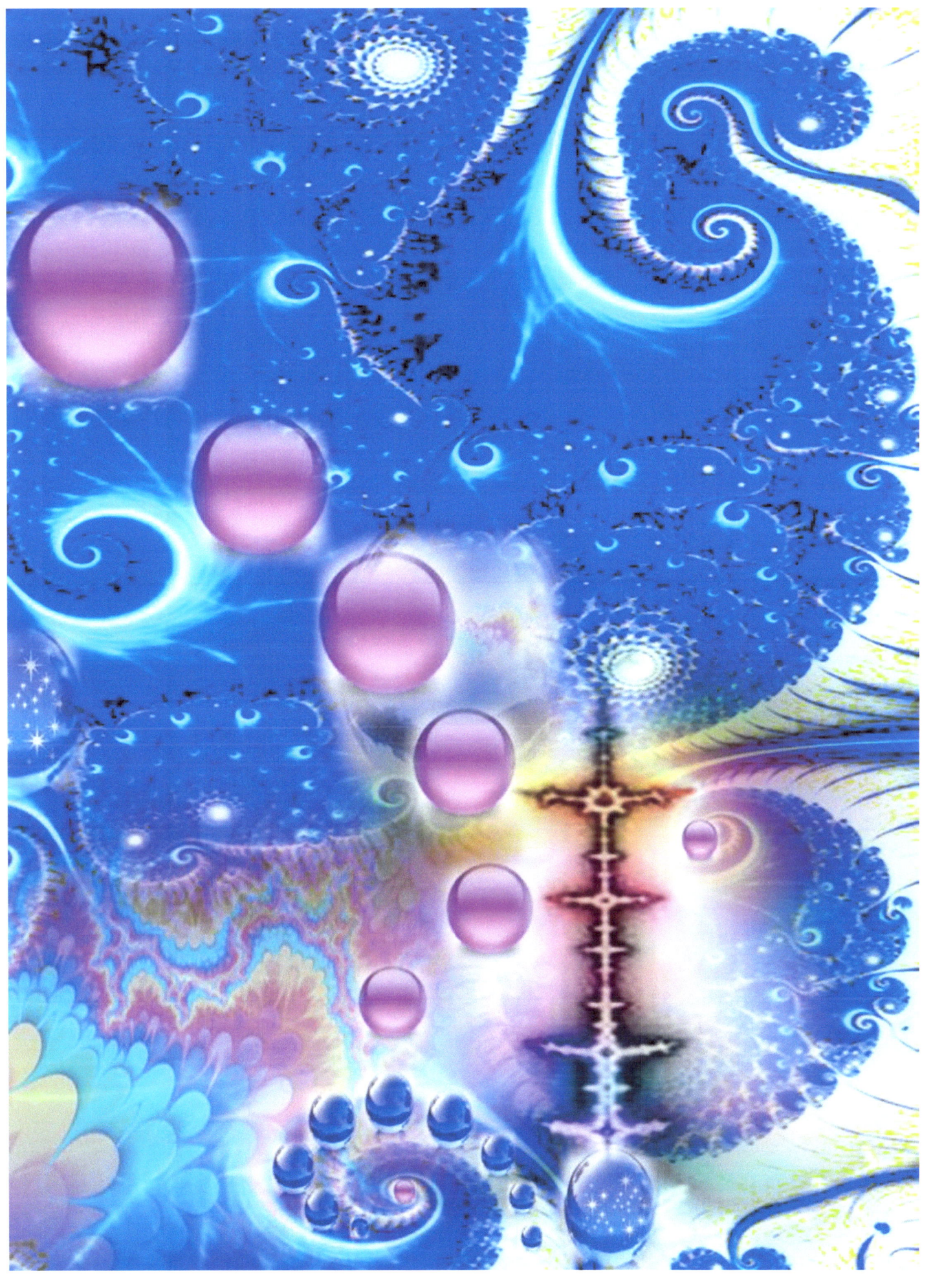

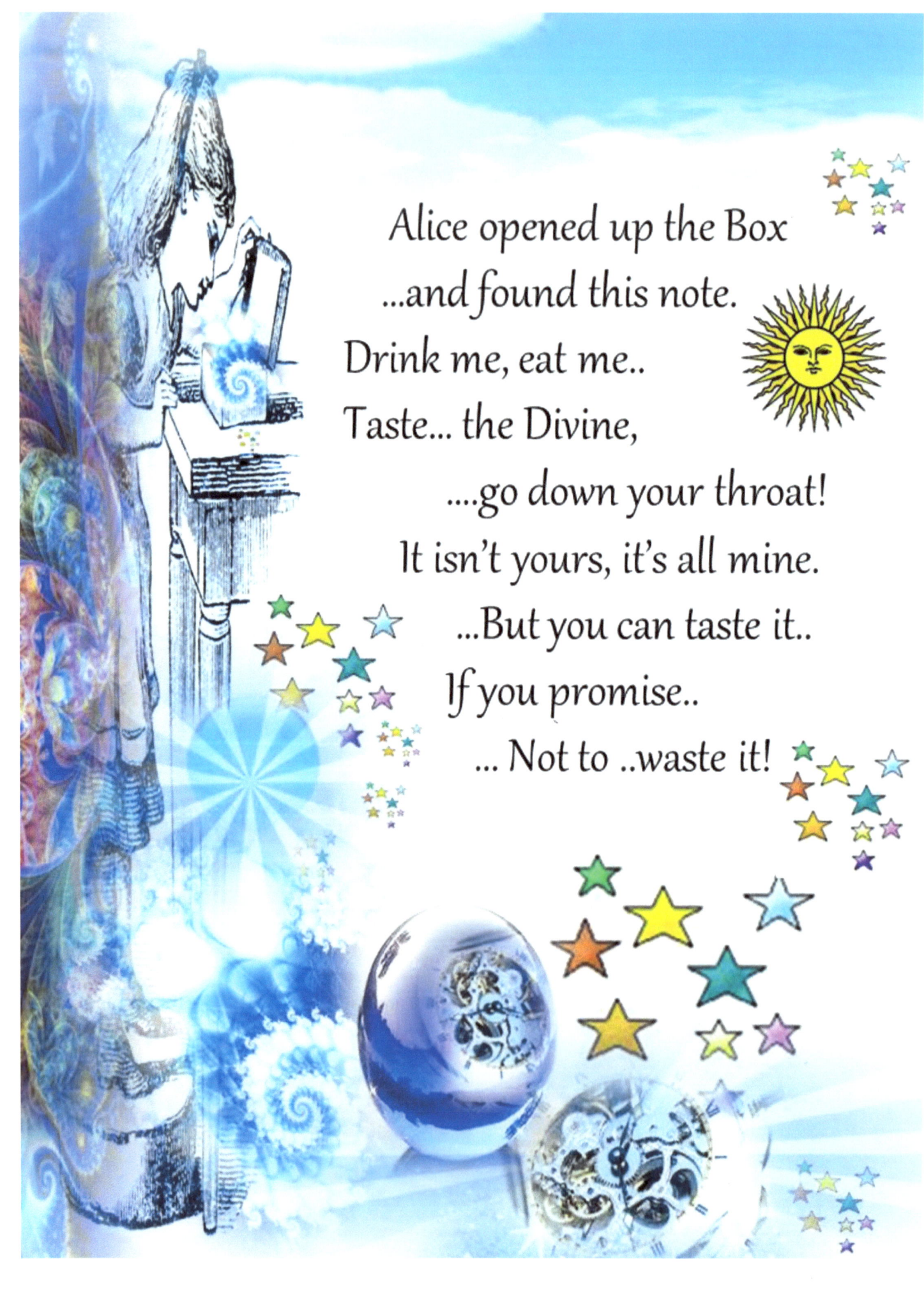

Alice opened up the Box
...and found this note.
Drink me, eat me..
Taste... the Divine,
....go down your throat!
It isn't yours, it's all mine.
...But you can taste it..
If you promise..
... Not to ..waste it!

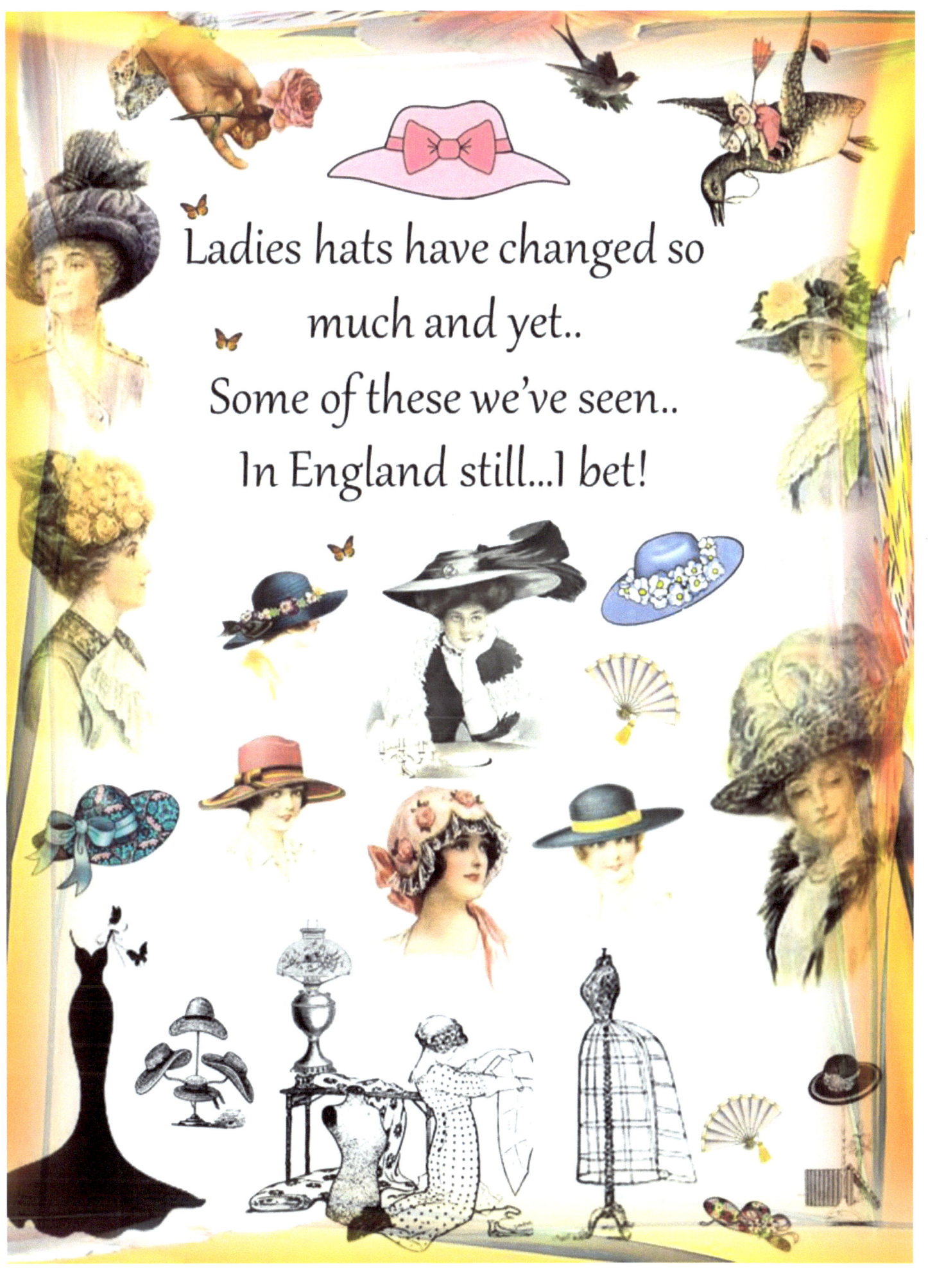

Ladies hats have changed so
much and yet..
Some of these we've seen..
In England still...I bet!

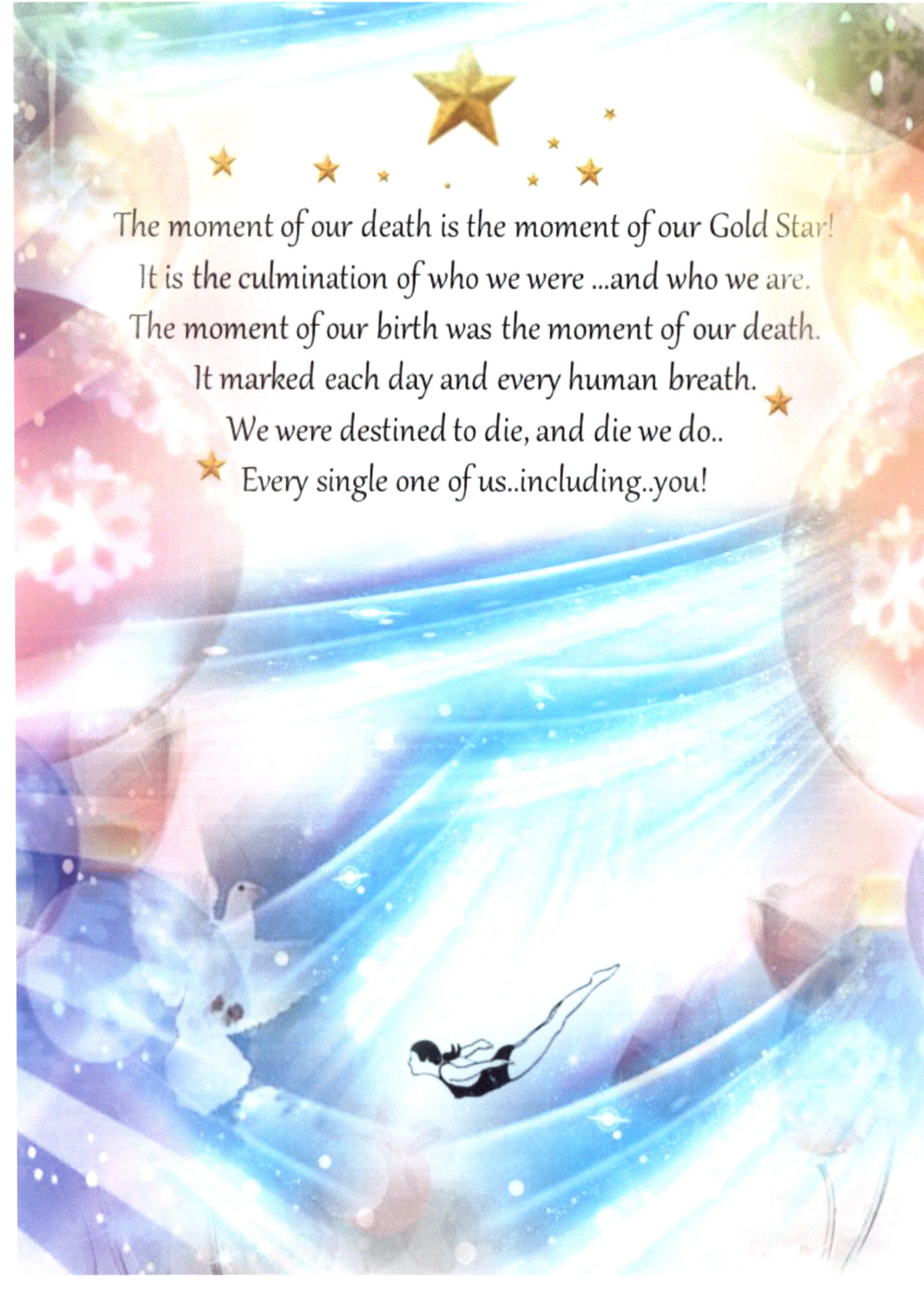

The moment of our death is the moment of our Gold Star!
It is the culmination of who we were ...and who we are.
The moment of our birth was the moment of our death.
It marked each day and every human breath.
We were destined to die, and die we do..
Every single one of us..including..you!

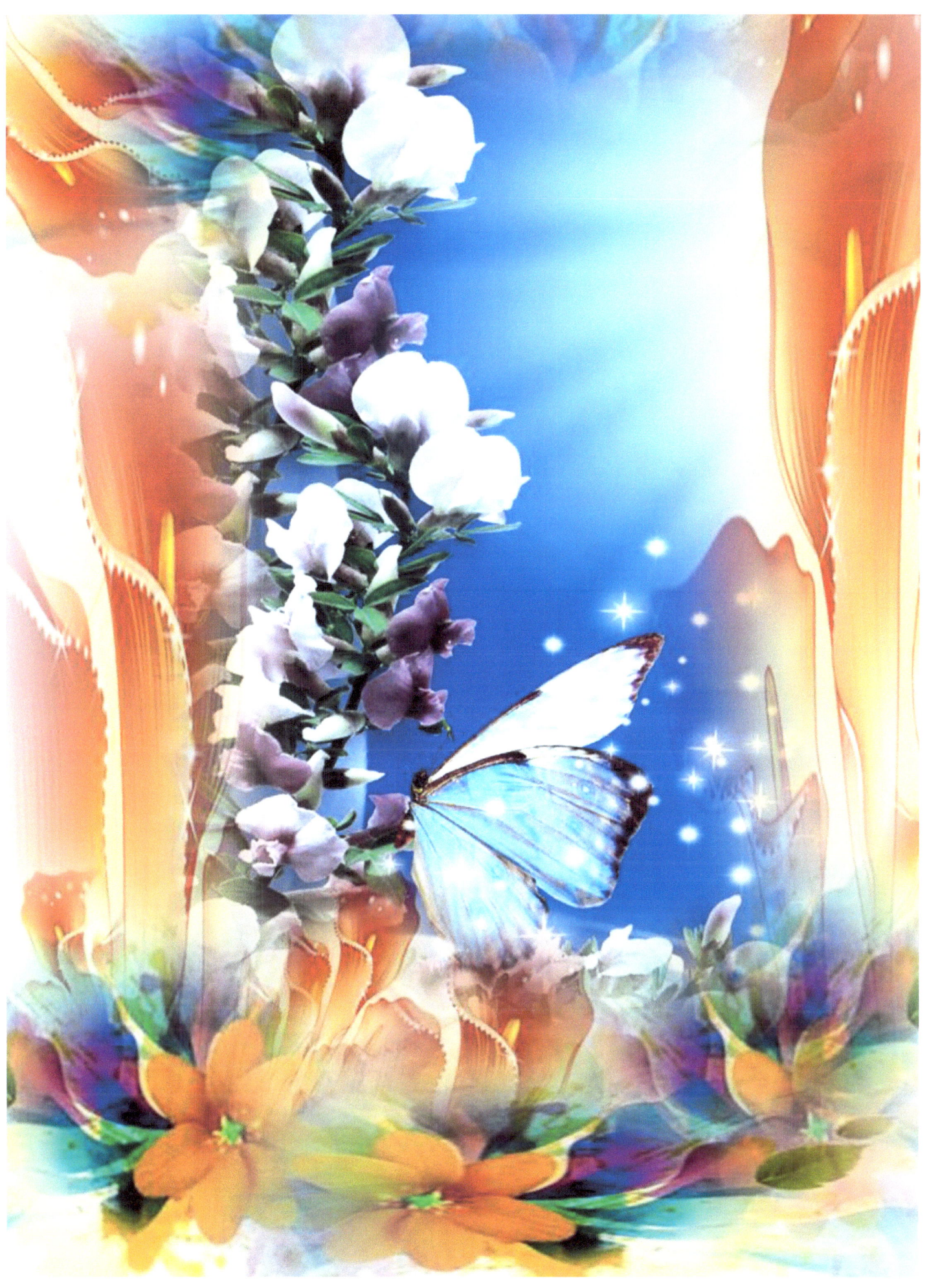

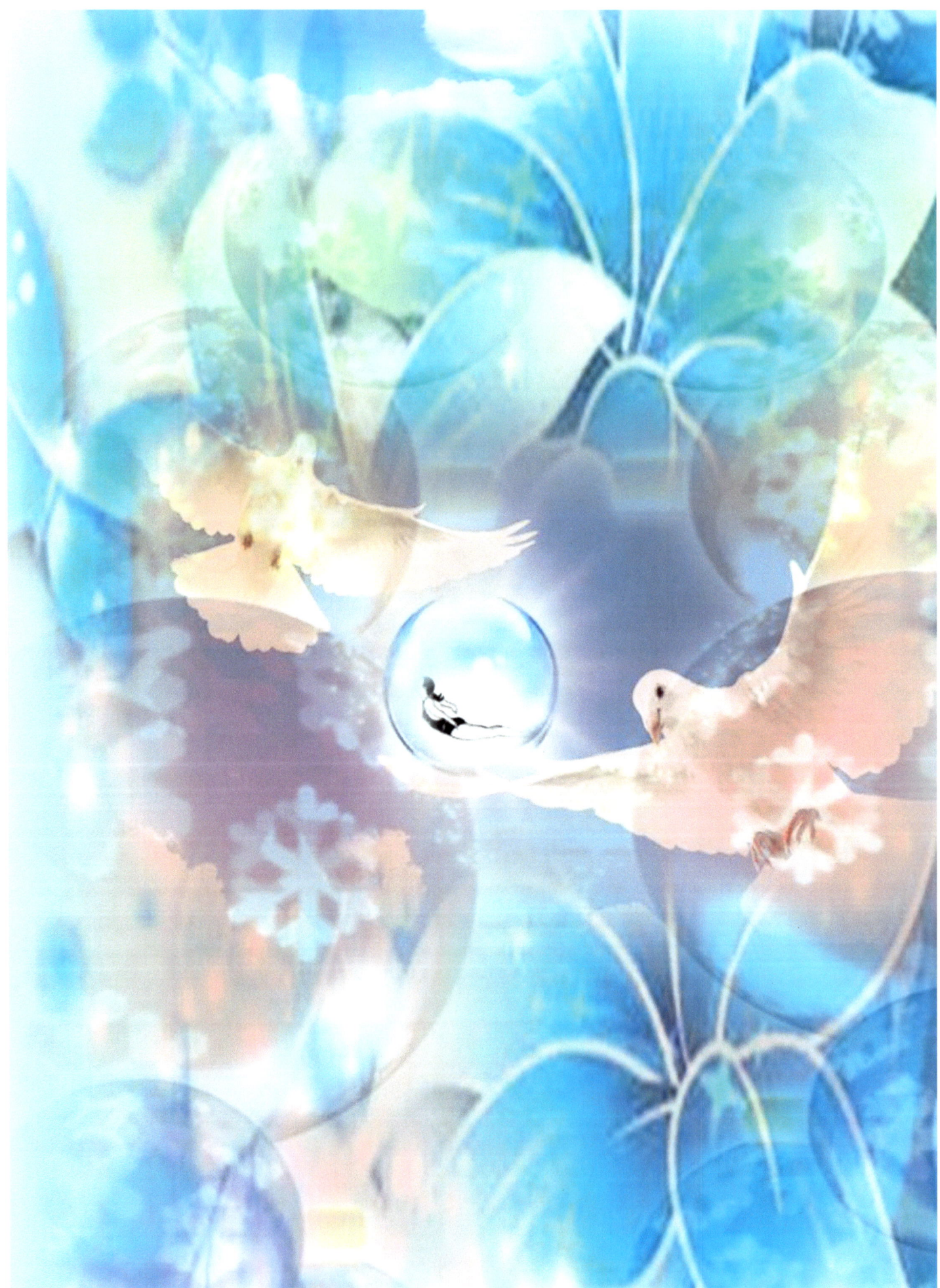

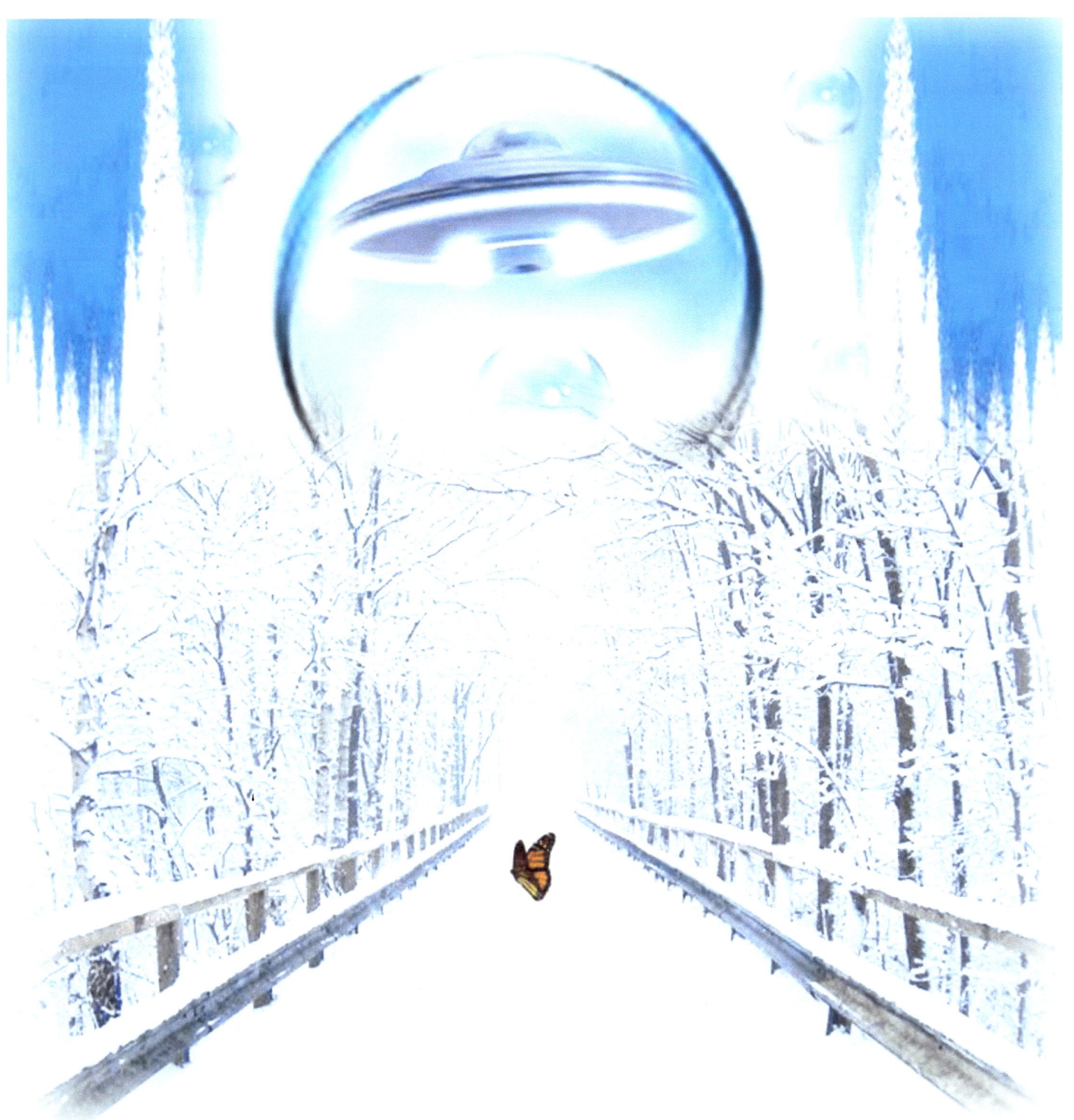

God is a being of supreme intelligence and science!
He's all about the laws of nature and scientific compliance!
One has only to look at the flight of the Butterfly..
Observe their state of perfection, and you'll see why!

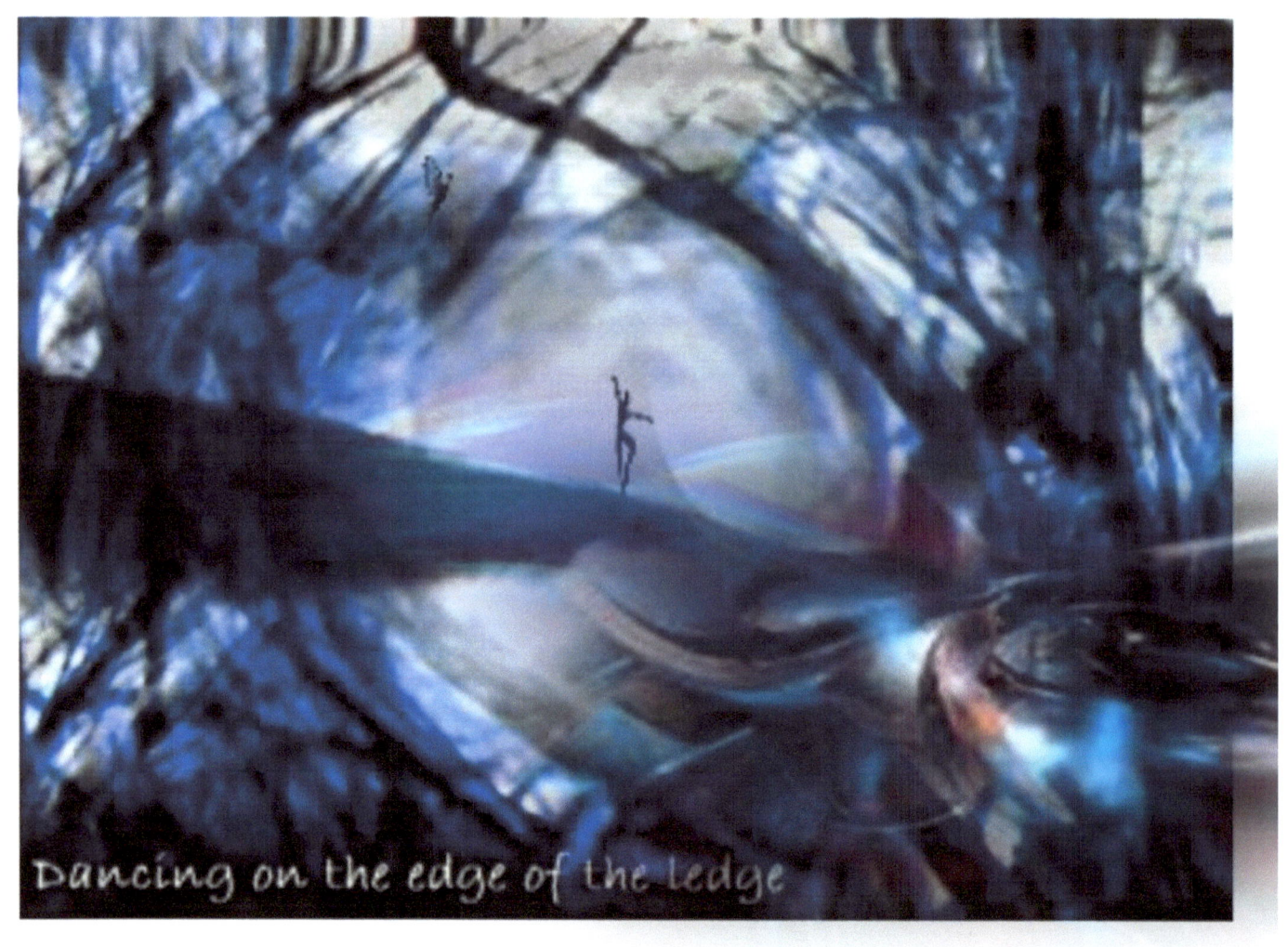

Dancing on the edge of the ledge

We are all dancing on the edge of the ledge.

The difference in today's world is this..

Someone is supposed to have your back if you fall. Someone

is supposed to lend you a hand so you don't fall.

And you are supposed to be there when they need a

helping hand too. So what happened?

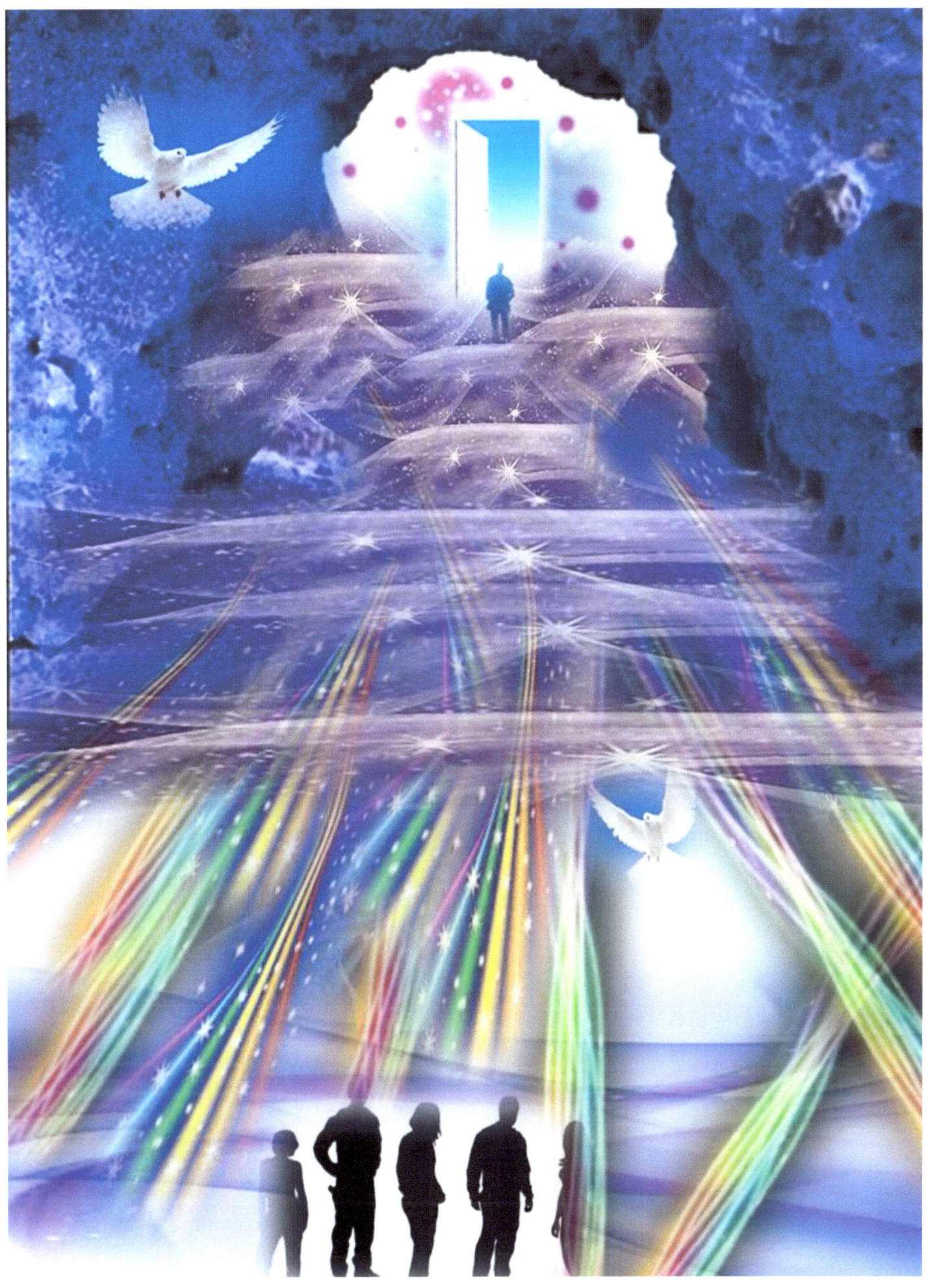

All of us find ourselves in dark waters at times...How we deal with these circumstances determines our destinies. Some of us will help the others. Some of us will help some of the others in their time of need.. Some of us will help only themselves. Which of these are you? Know Thyself! :)

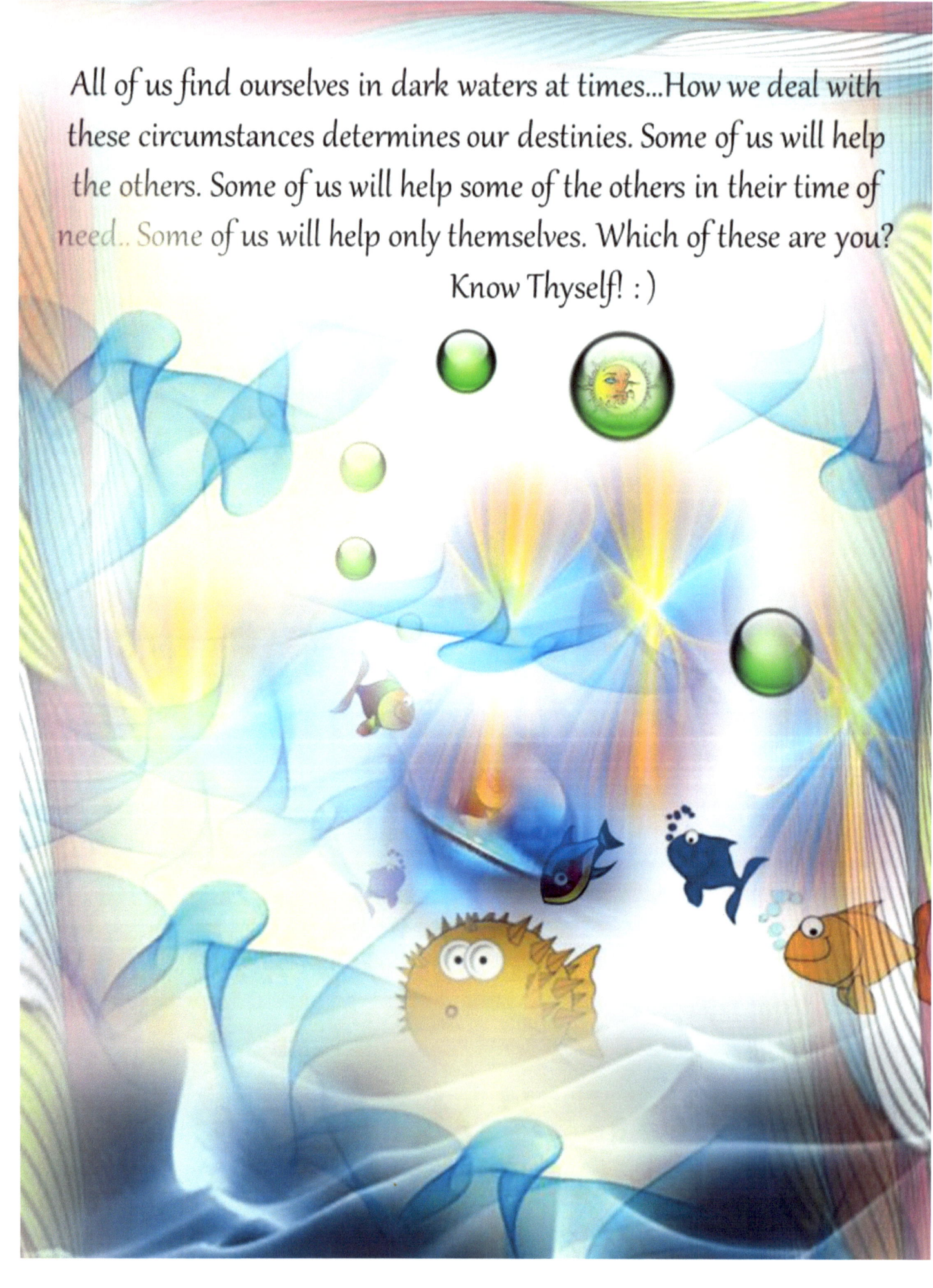

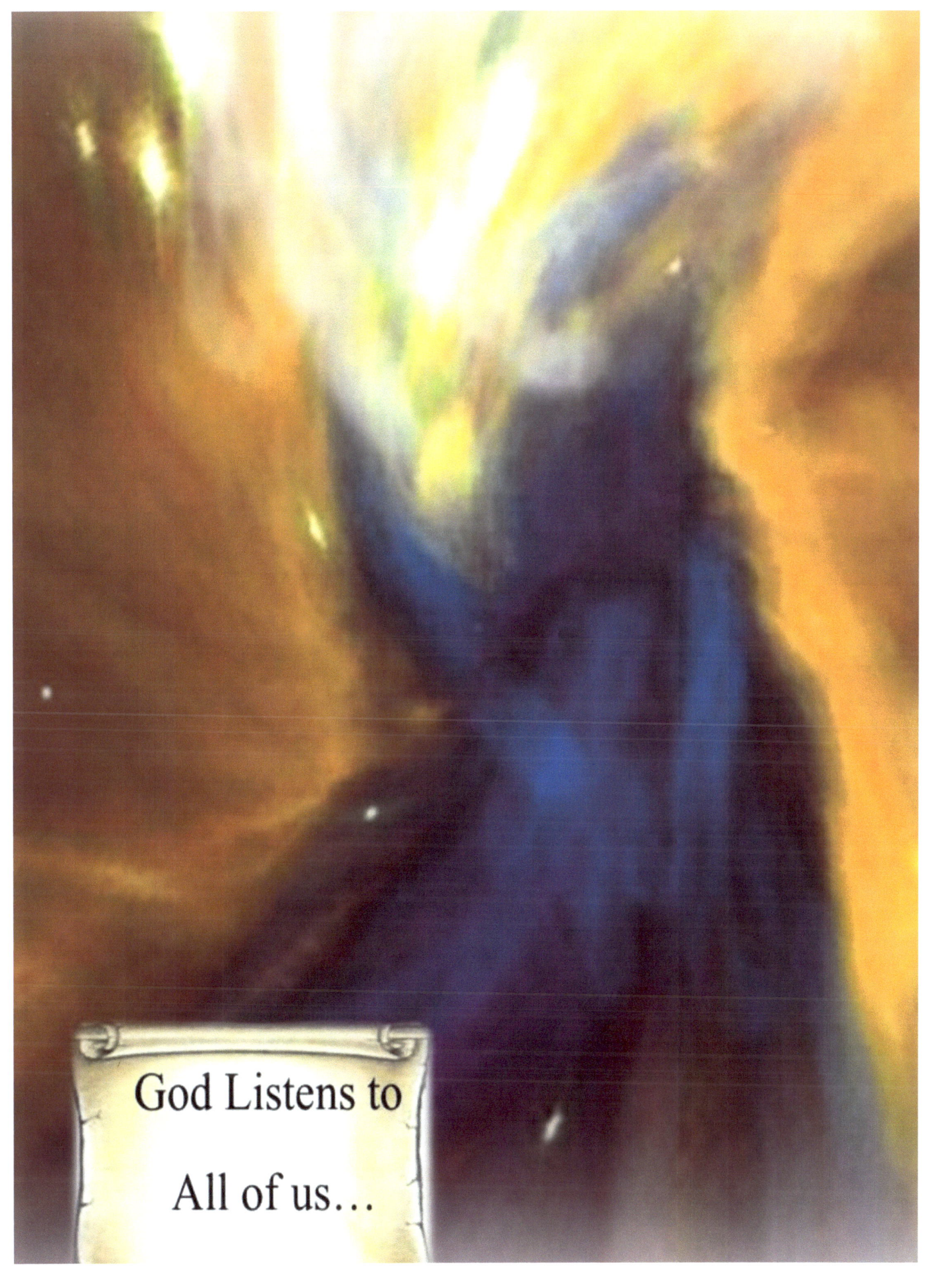

God Listens to

All of us…

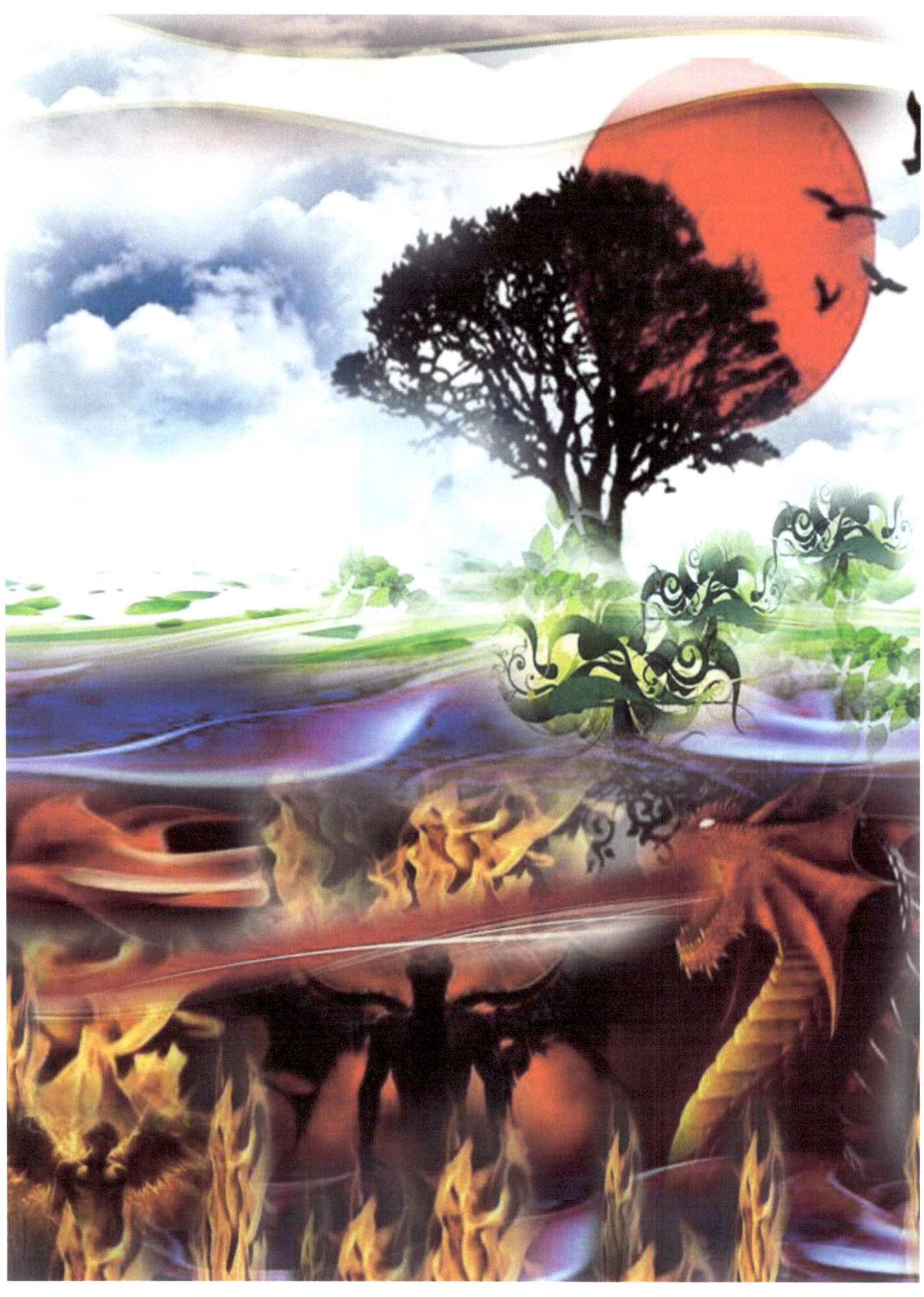

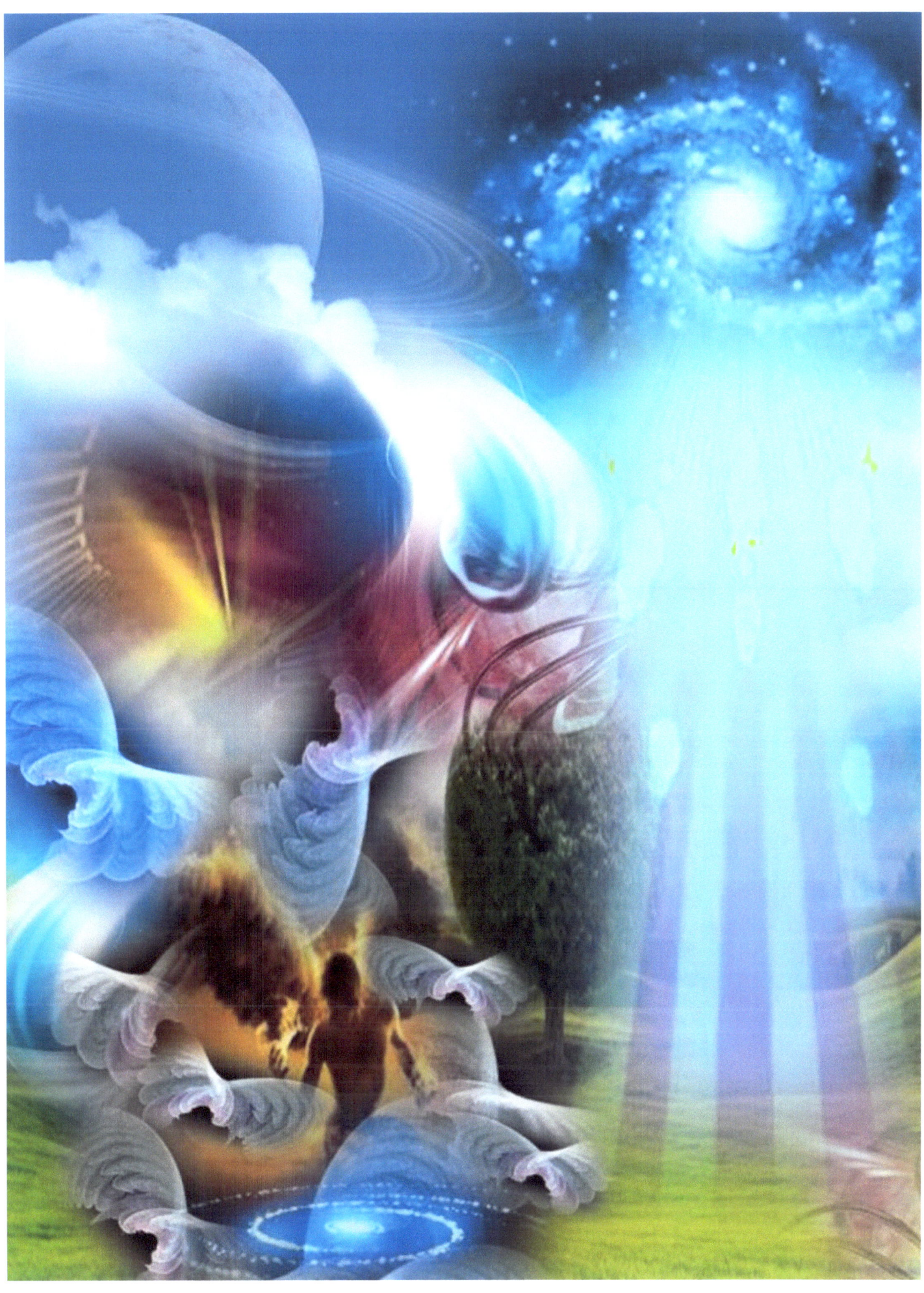

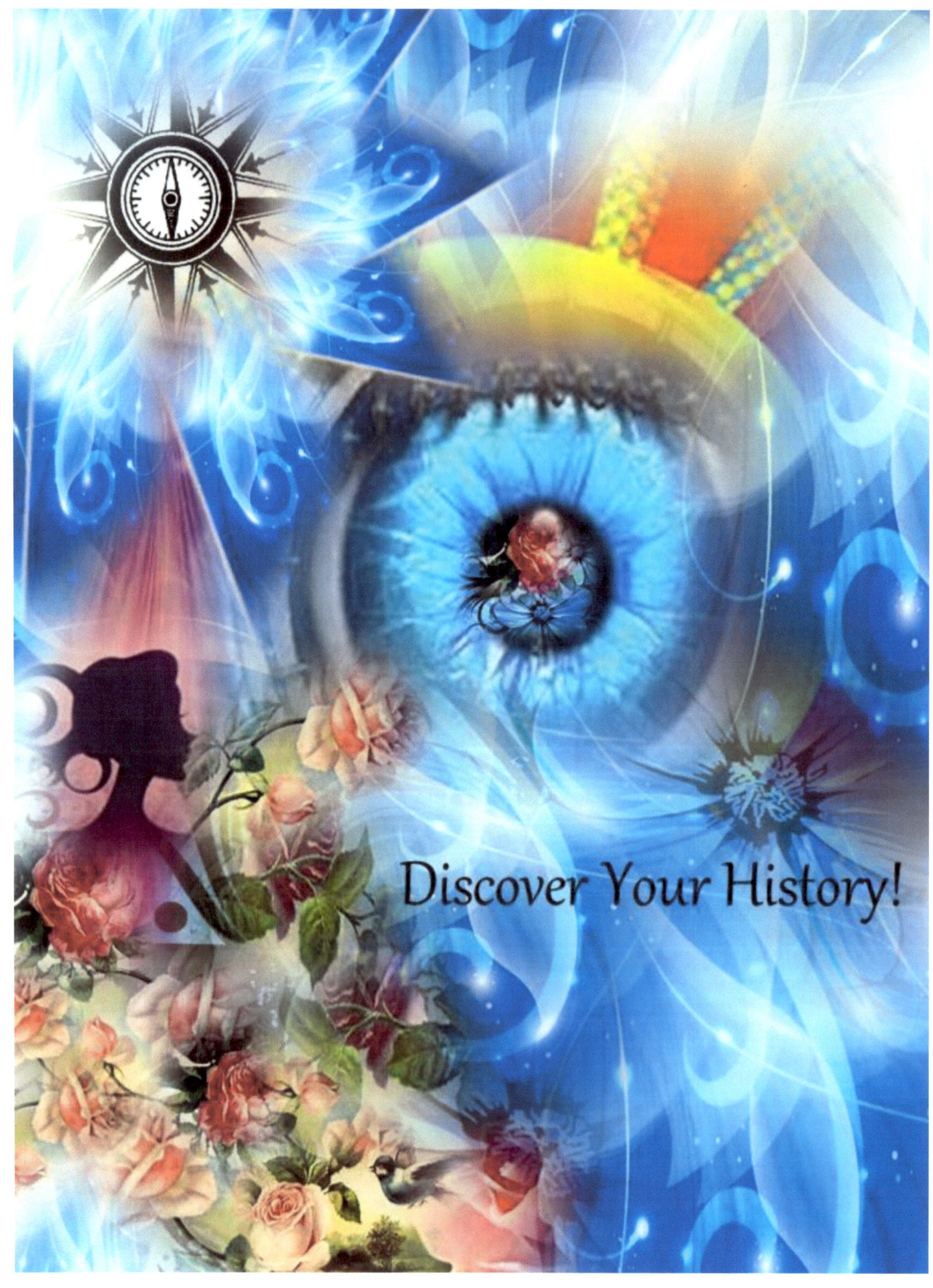

Discover Your History!

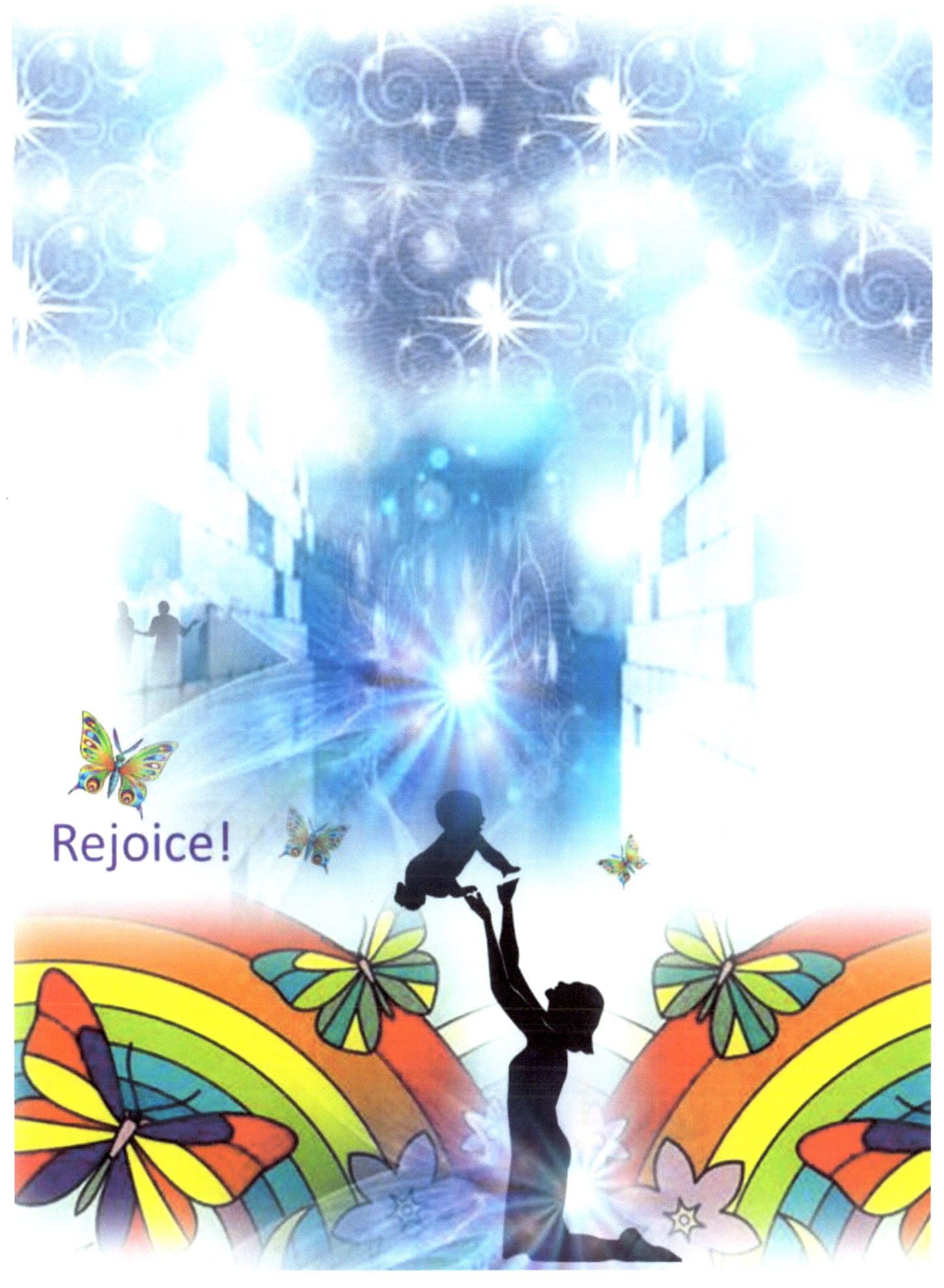

Rejoice!

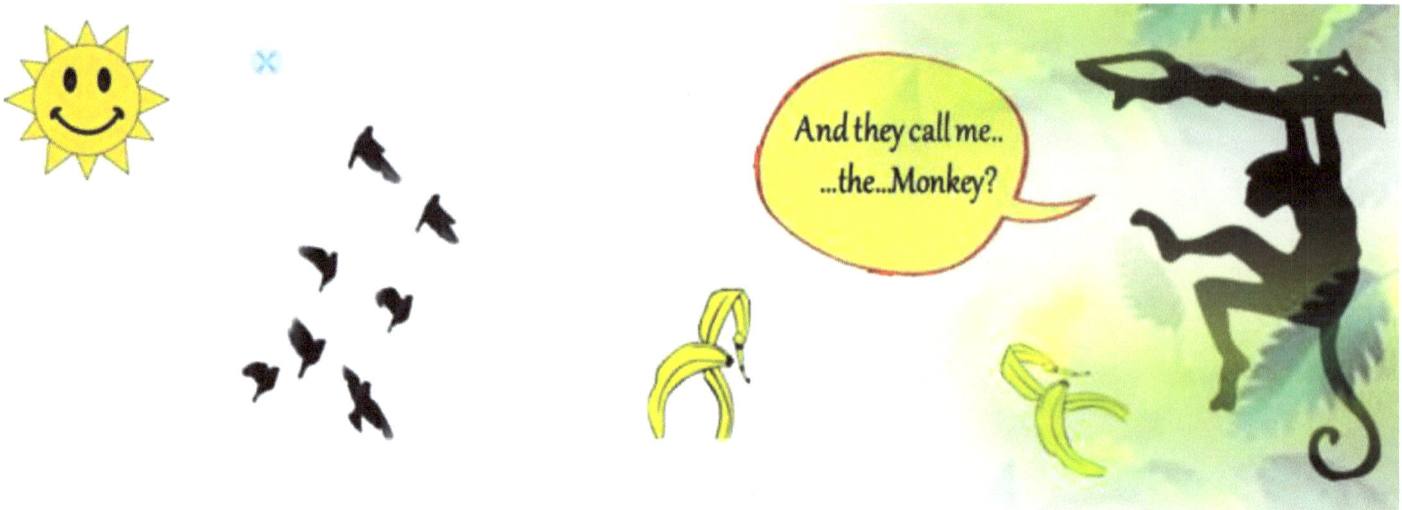

And they call me..
...the...Monkey?

In all these years, I would have thought more than just our appearance would have evolved.

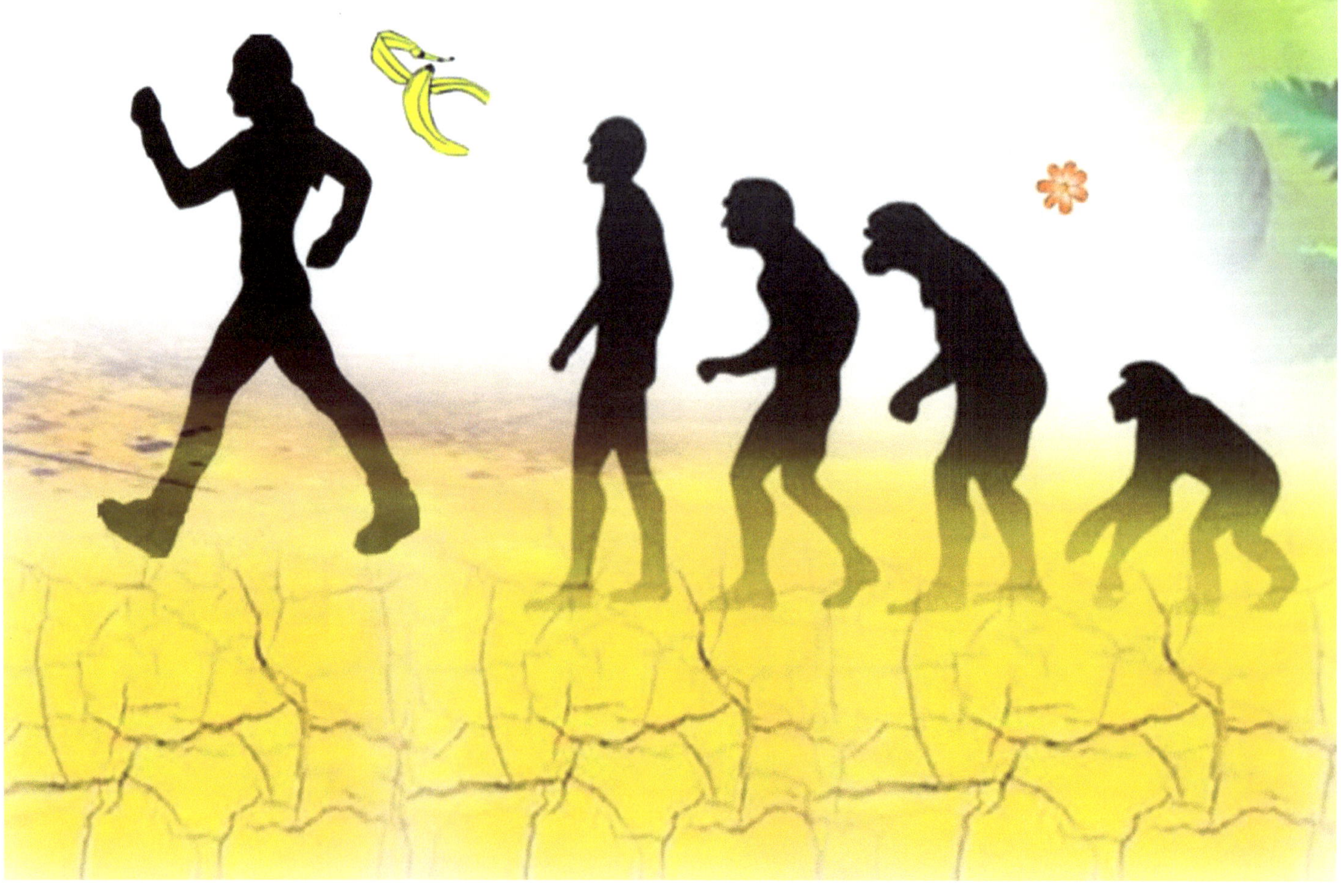

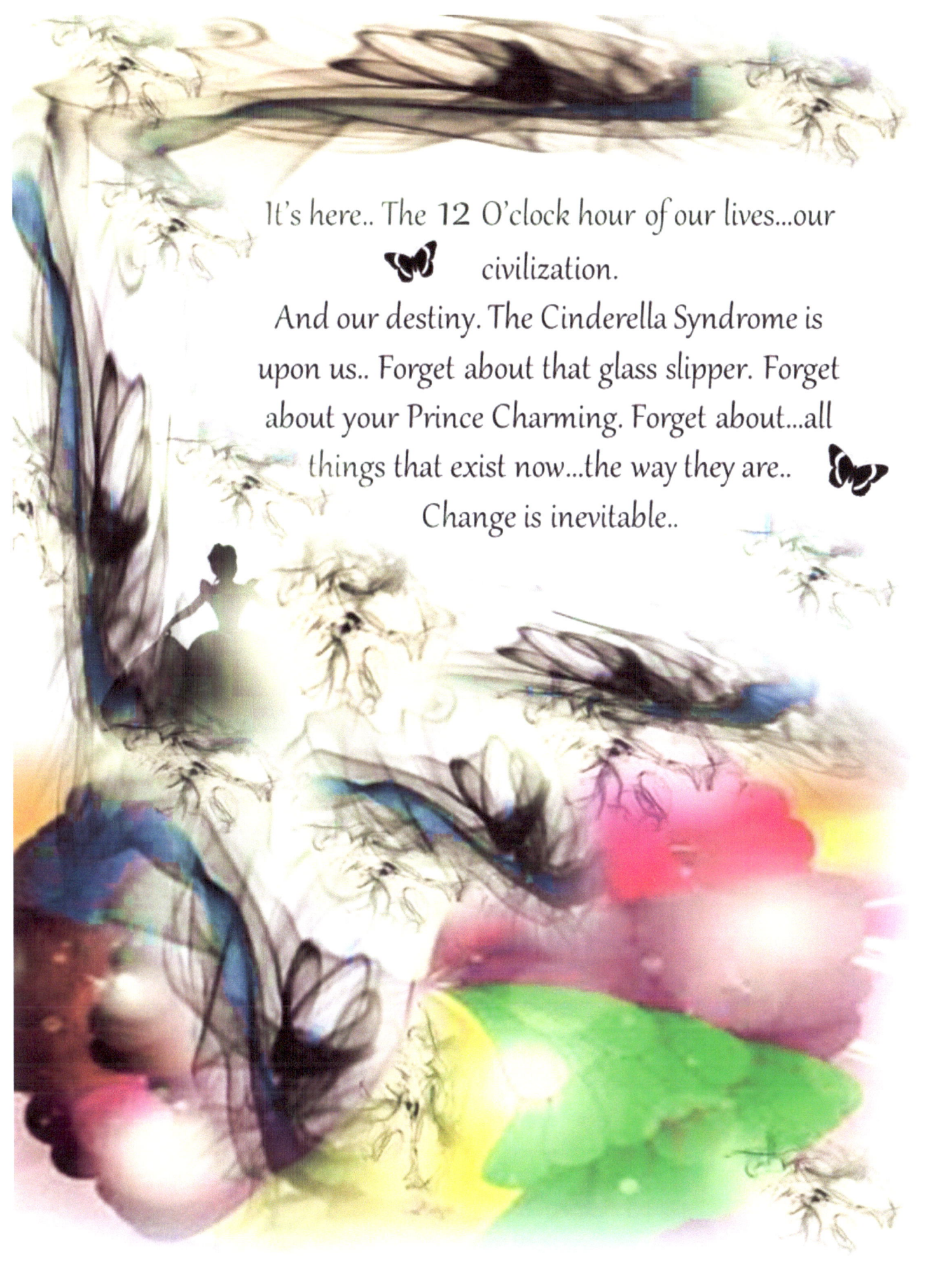

It's here.. The 12 O'clock hour of our lives...our civilization.

And our destiny. The Cinderella Syndrome is upon us.. Forget about that glass slipper. Forget about your Prince Charming. Forget about...all things that exist now...the way they are.. Change is inevitable..

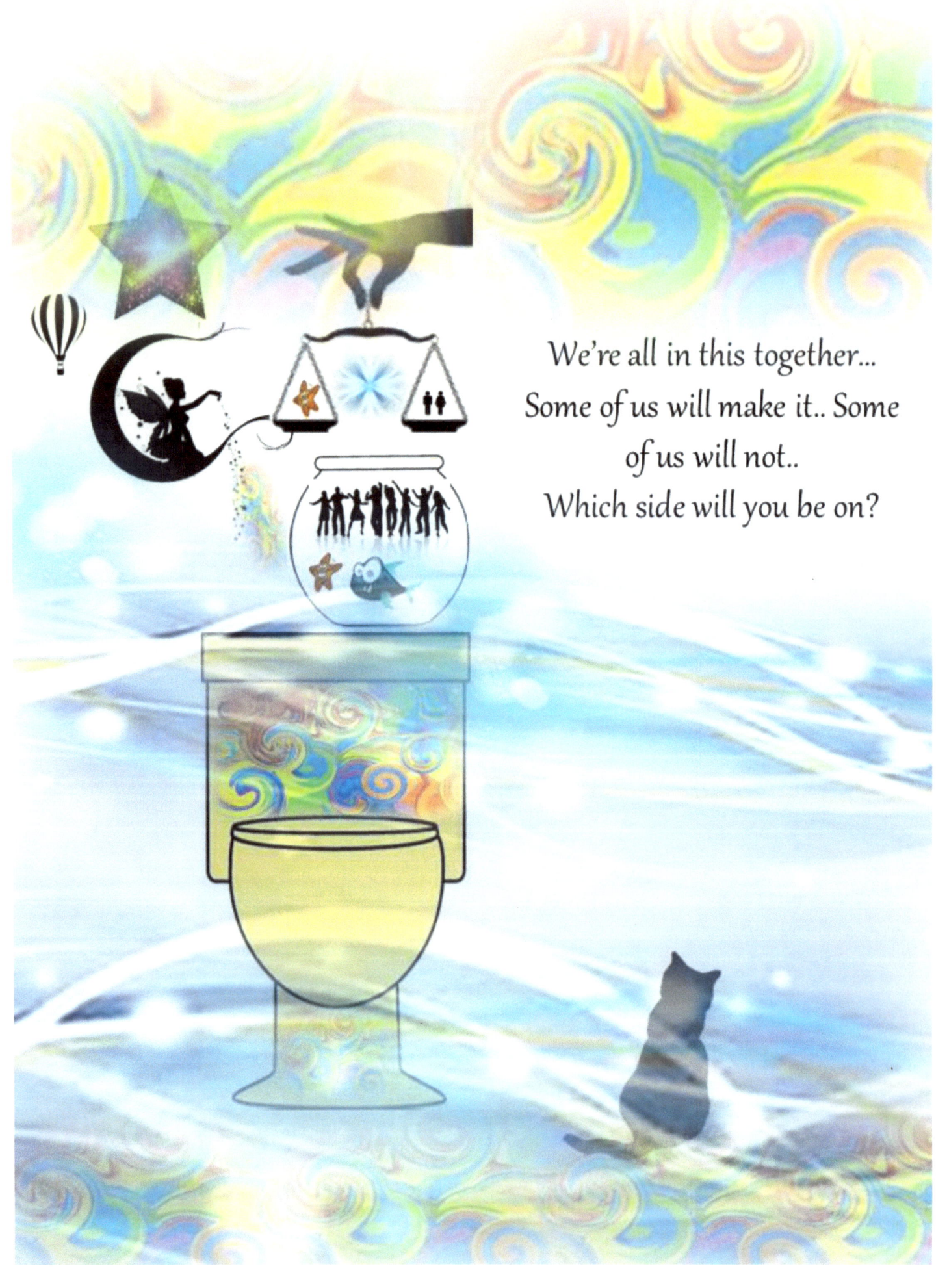

We're all in this together...
Some of us will make it.. Some
of us will not..
Which side will you be on?

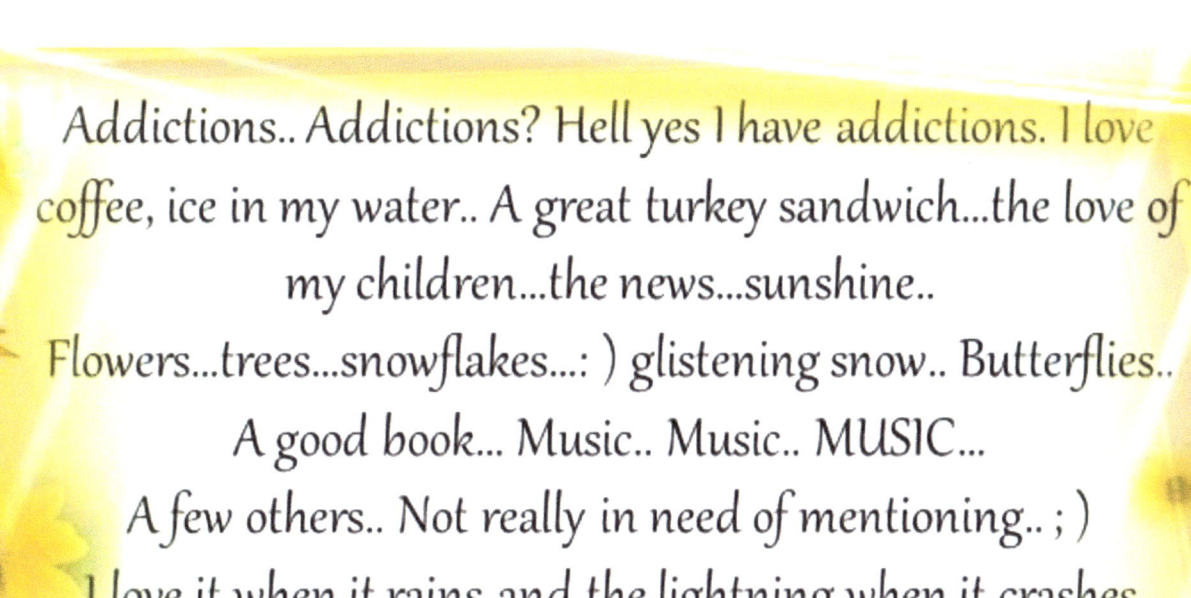

Addictions.. Addictions? Hell yes I have addictions. I love coffee, ice in my water.. A great turkey sandwich...the love of my children...the news...sunshine..
Flowers...trees...snowflakes...:) glistening snow.. Butterflies..
A good book... Music.. Music.. MUSIC...
A few others.. Not really in need of mentioning.. ;)
I love it when it rains and the lightning when it crashes unexpectantly in the sky.. Love Holidays.. Christmas morning when the kids see their gifts...God when he visits the church on Christmas Eve.. and the people actually act like humans... All animals.. And children. I am addicted to the wonders of Nature and the possibilities all around us! I love a good movie, and I love ..to be kissed when I least expect it.. From those I love. I love when people ...love each other...who doesn't?
Oh..and I love chocolate, flowers and chicken soup!

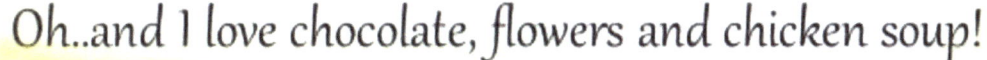

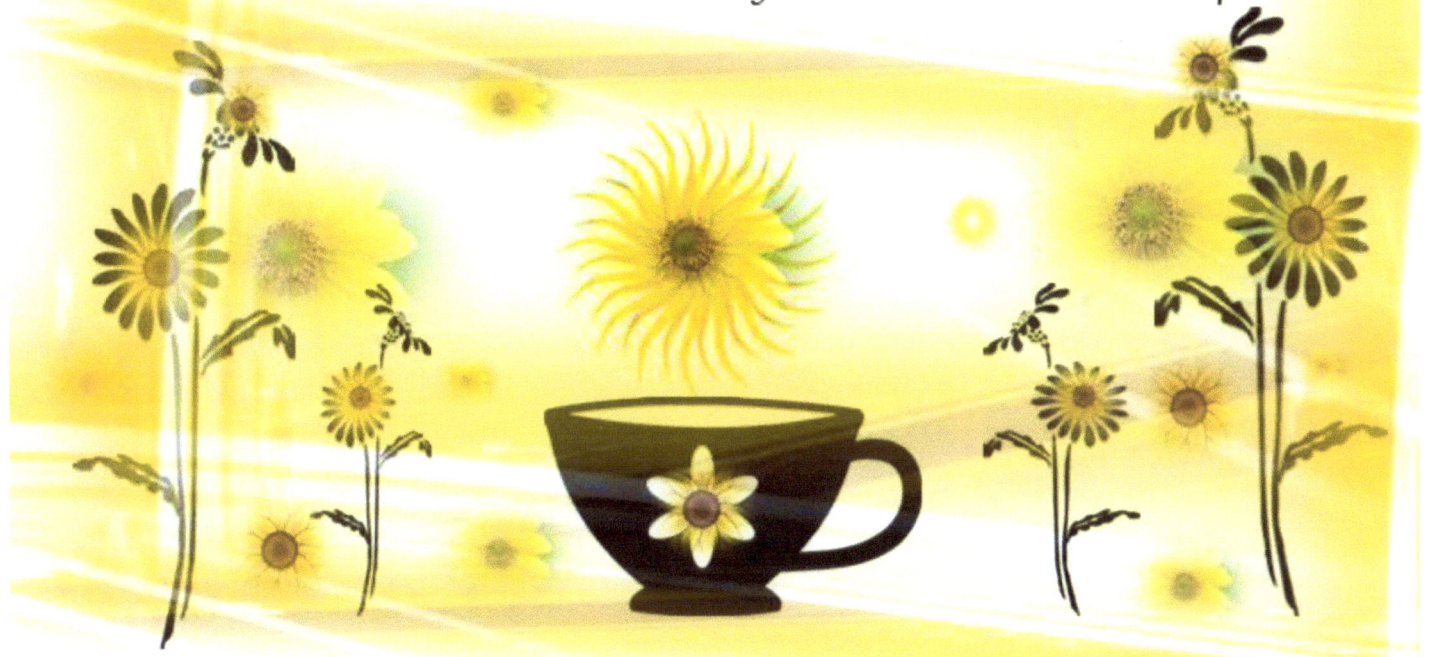

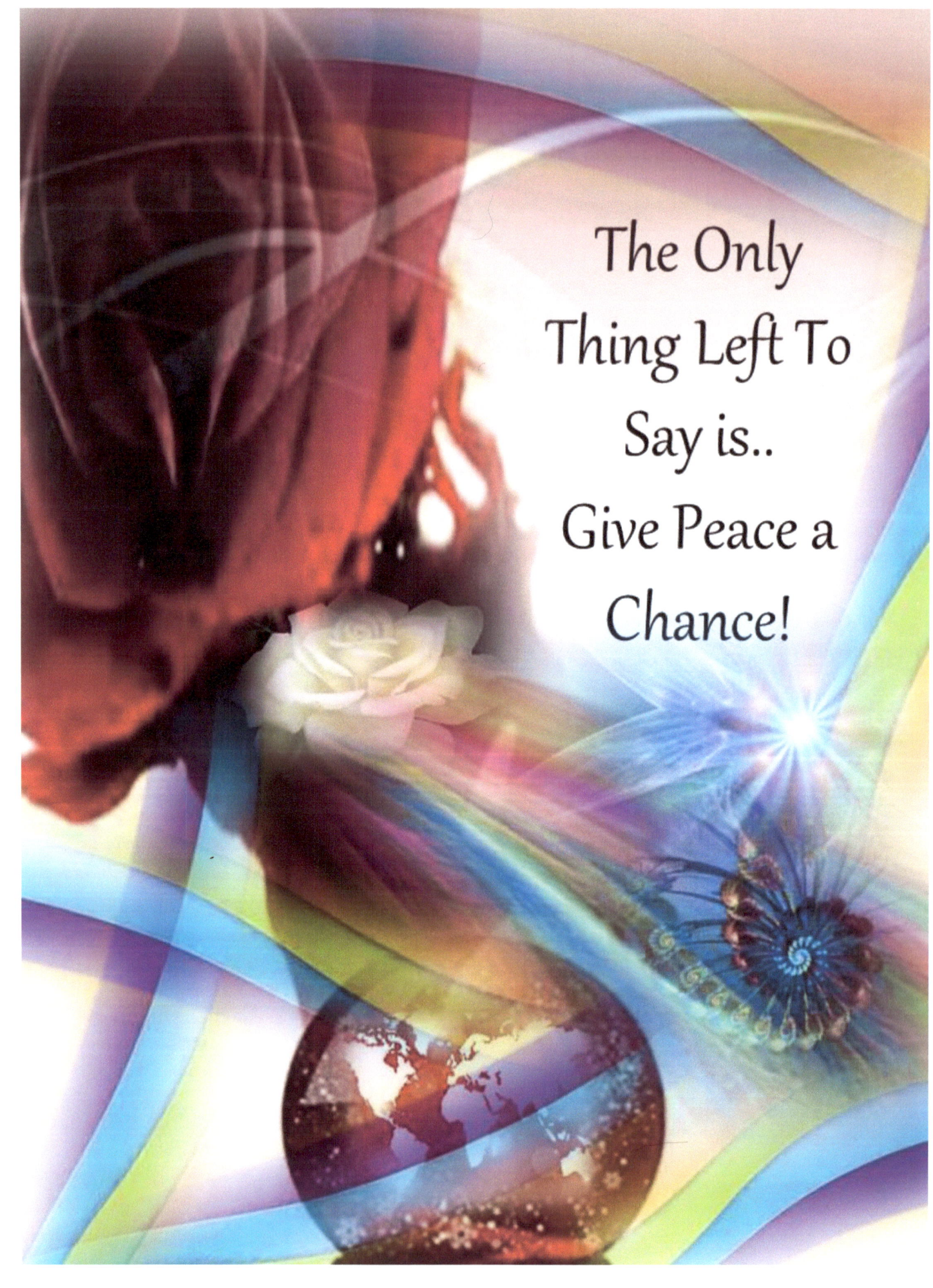

The Only
Thing Left To
Say is..
Give Peace a
Chance!

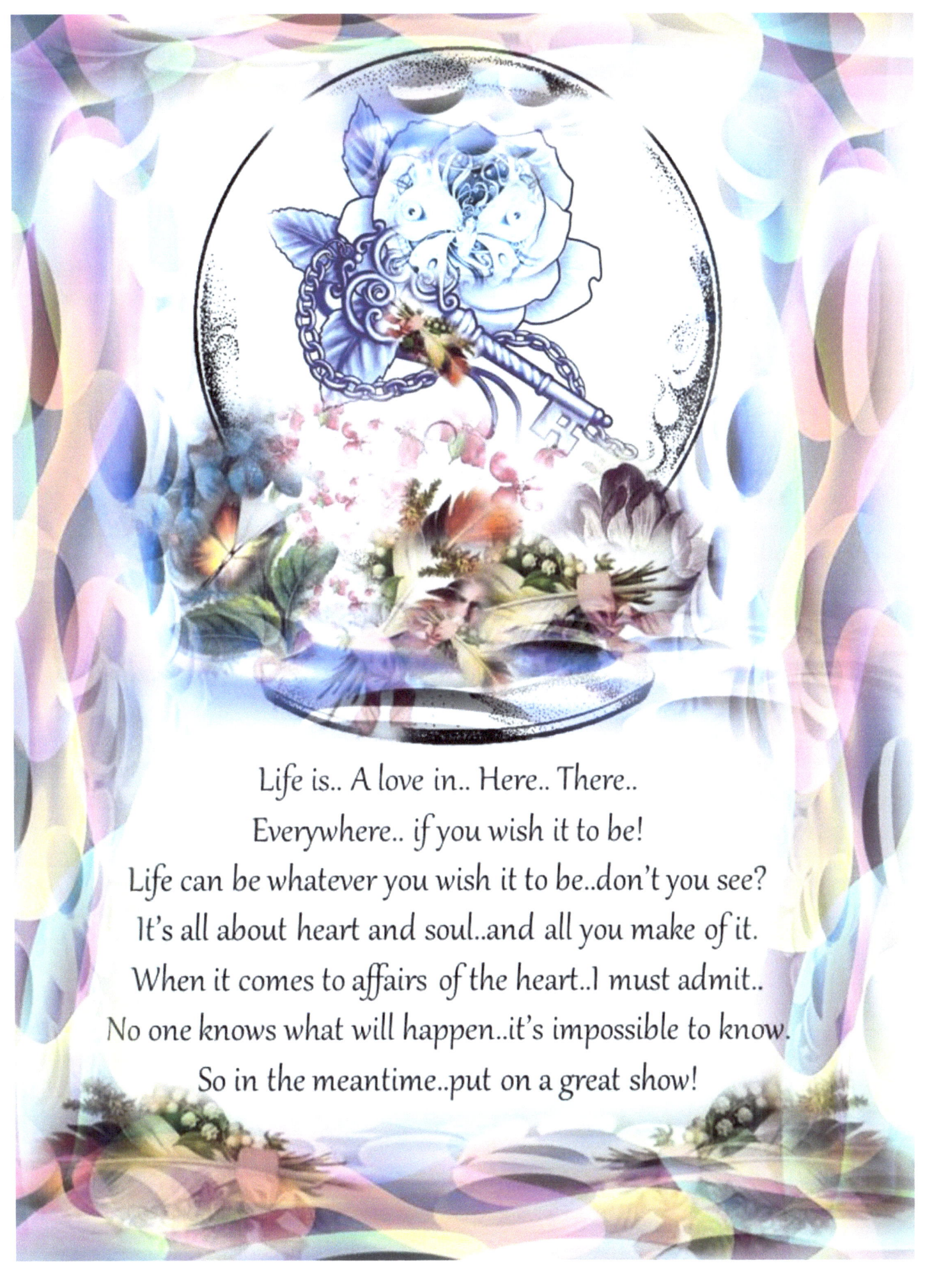

Life is.. A love in.. Here.. There..
Everywhere.. if you wish it to be!
Life can be whatever you wish it to be..don't you see?
It's all about heart and soul..and all you make of it.
When it comes to affairs of the heart..I must admit..
No one knows what will happen..it's impossible to know.
So in the meantime..put on a great show!

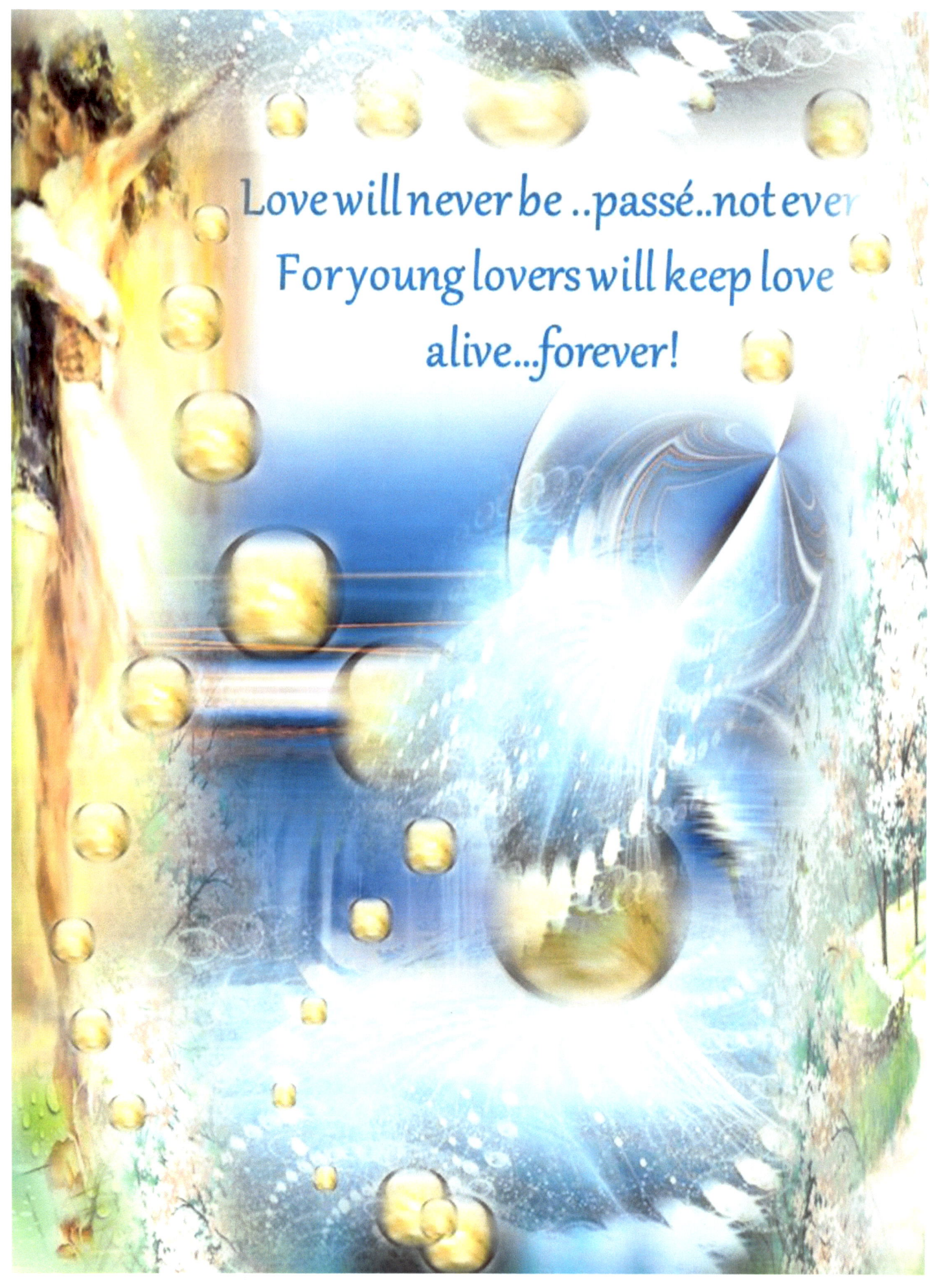

Love will never be ..passé..not ever
For young lovers will keep love
alive...forever!

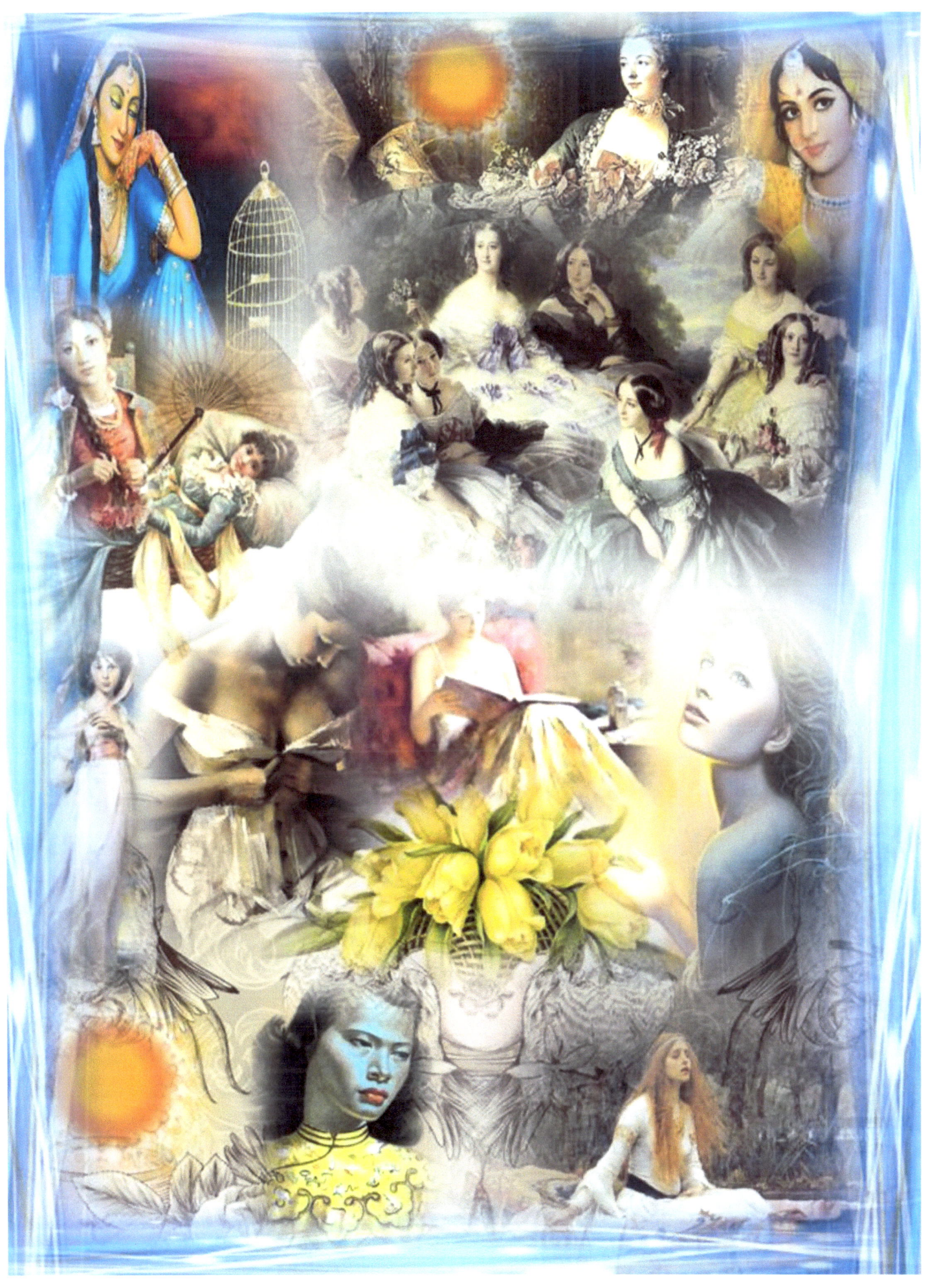

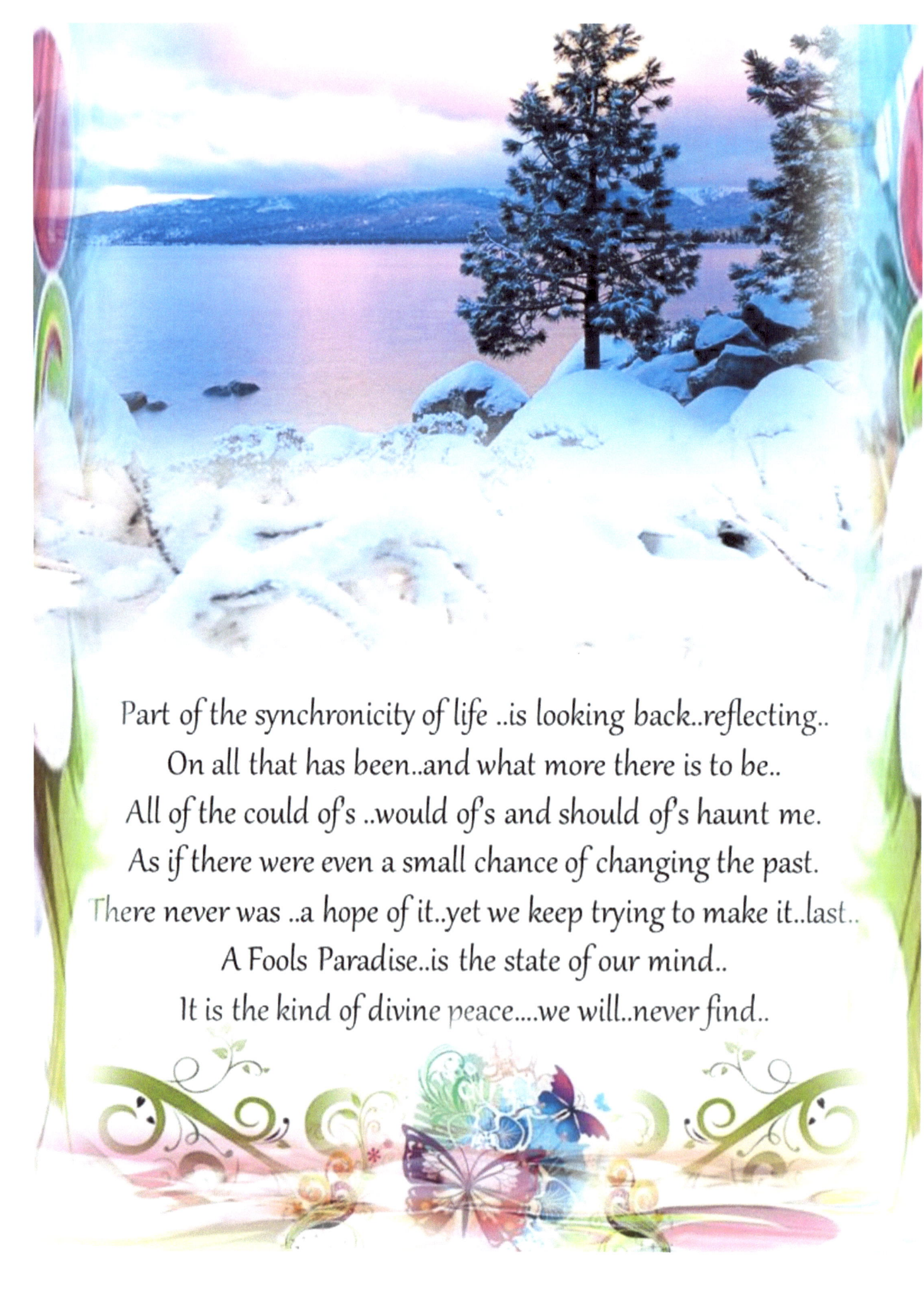

Part of the synchronicity of life ..is looking back..reflecting..

On all that has been..and what more there is to be..

All of the could of's ..would of's and should of's haunt me.

As if there were even a small chance of changing the past.

There never was ..a hope of it..yet we keep trying to make it..last..

A Fools Paradise..is the state of our mind..

It is the kind of divine peace....we will..never find..

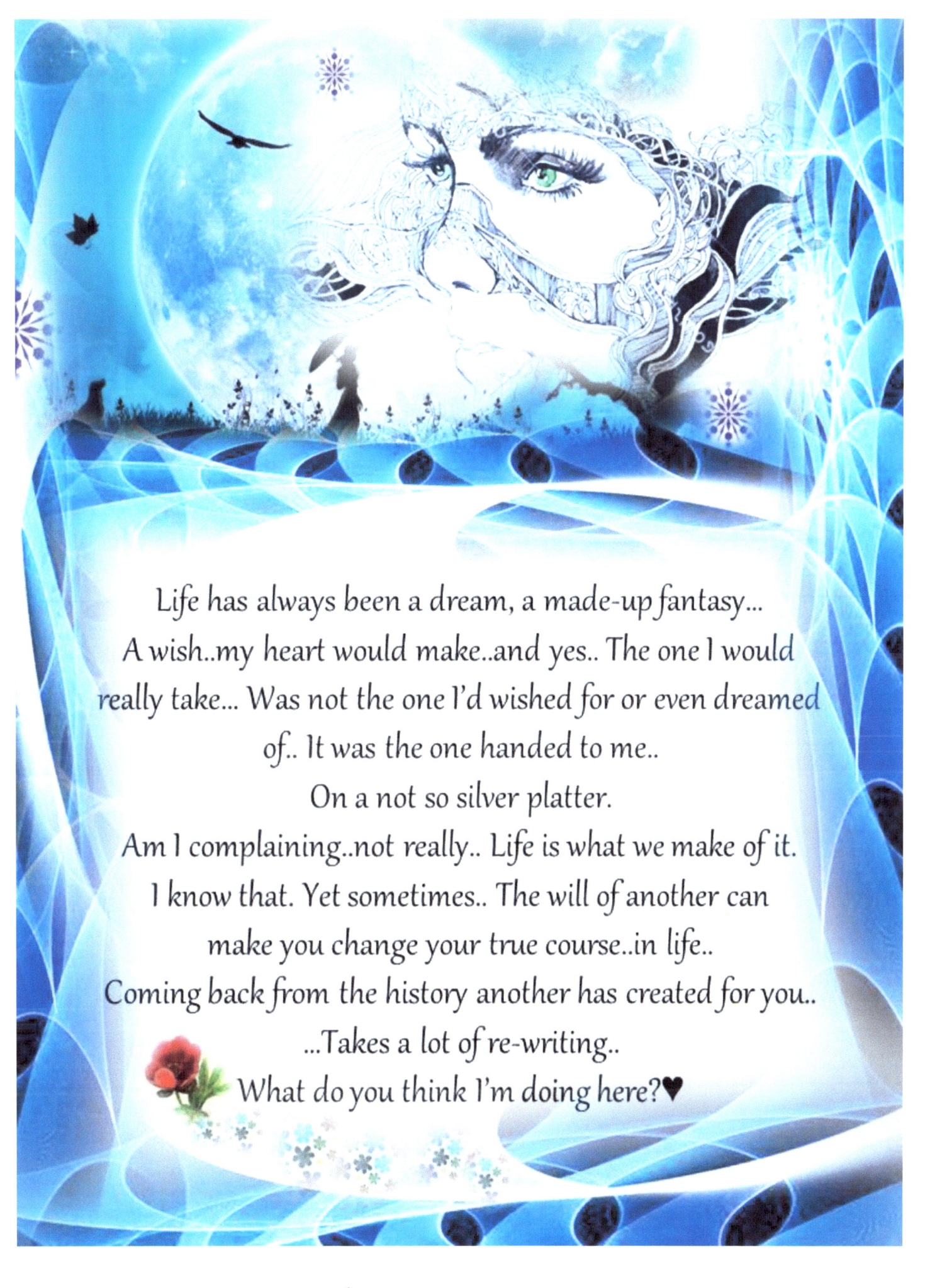

Life has always been a dream, a made-up fantasy...
A wish..my heart would make..and yes.. The one I would
really take... Was not the one I'd wished for or even dreamed
of.. It was the one handed to me..
On a not so silver platter.
Am I complaining..not really.. Life is what we make of it.
I know that. Yet sometimes.. The will of another can
make you change your true course..in life..
Coming back from the history another has created for you..
...Takes a lot of re-writing..
What do you think I'm doing here?♥

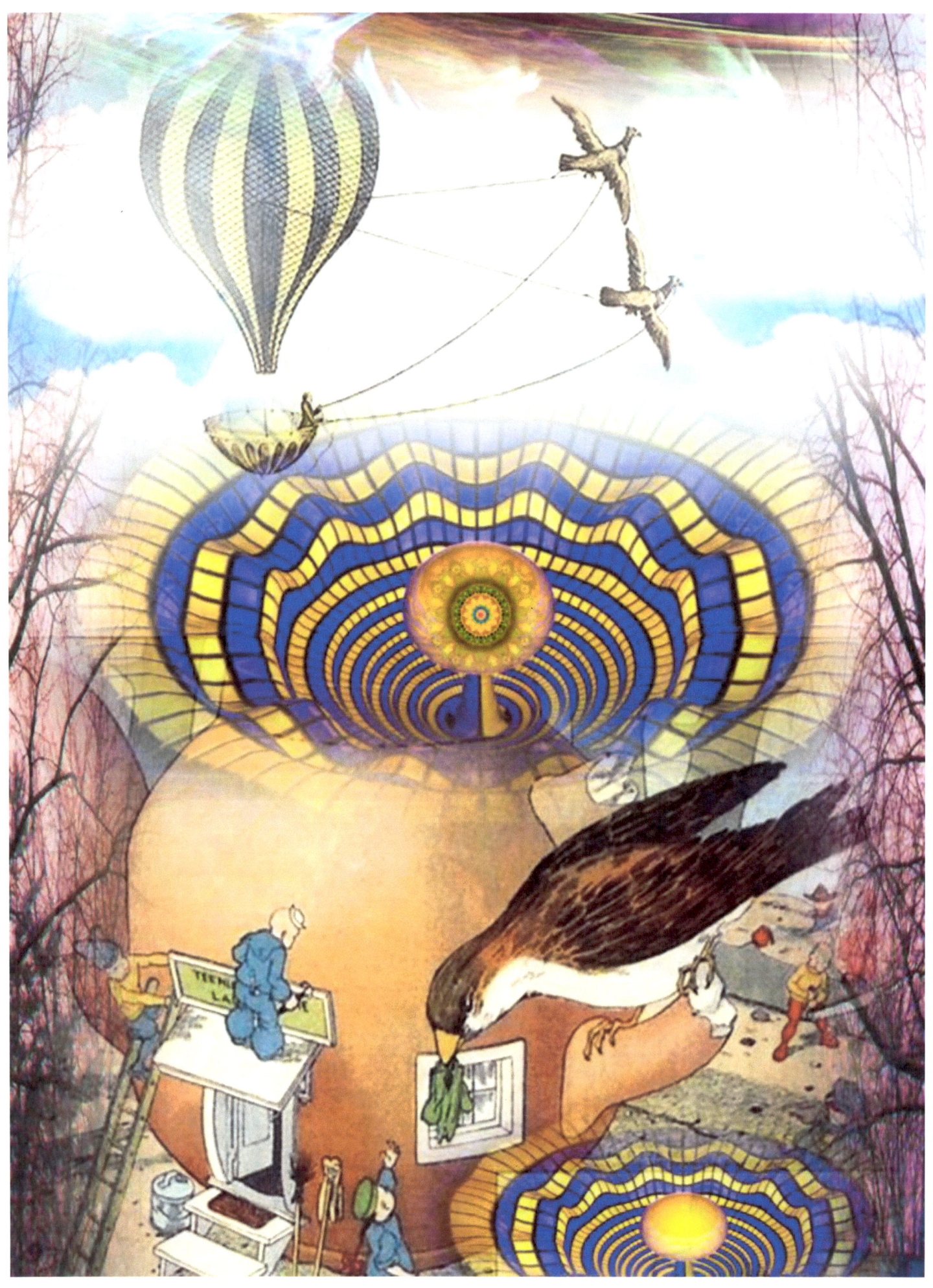

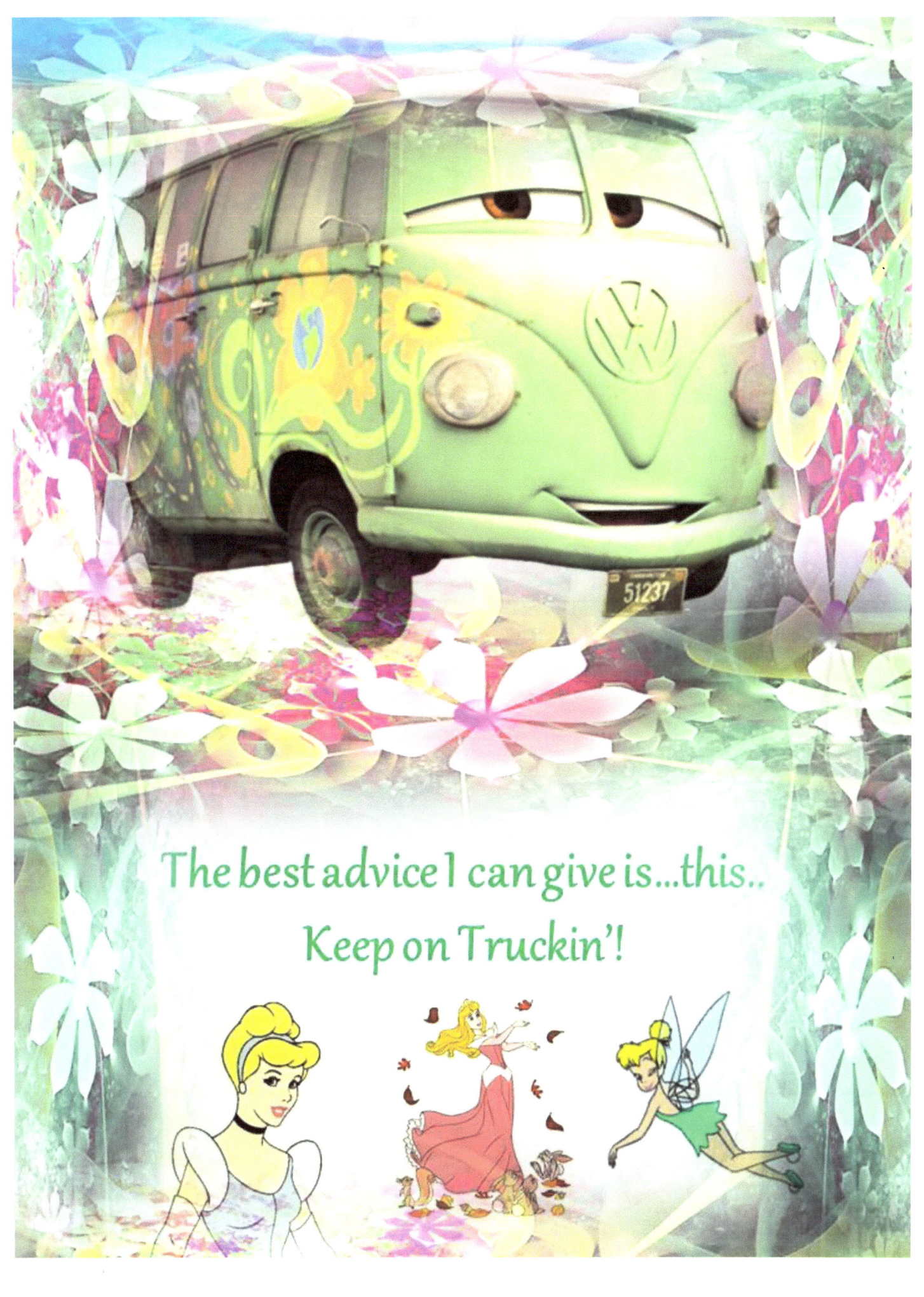

The best advice I can give is...this..
Keep on Truckin'!

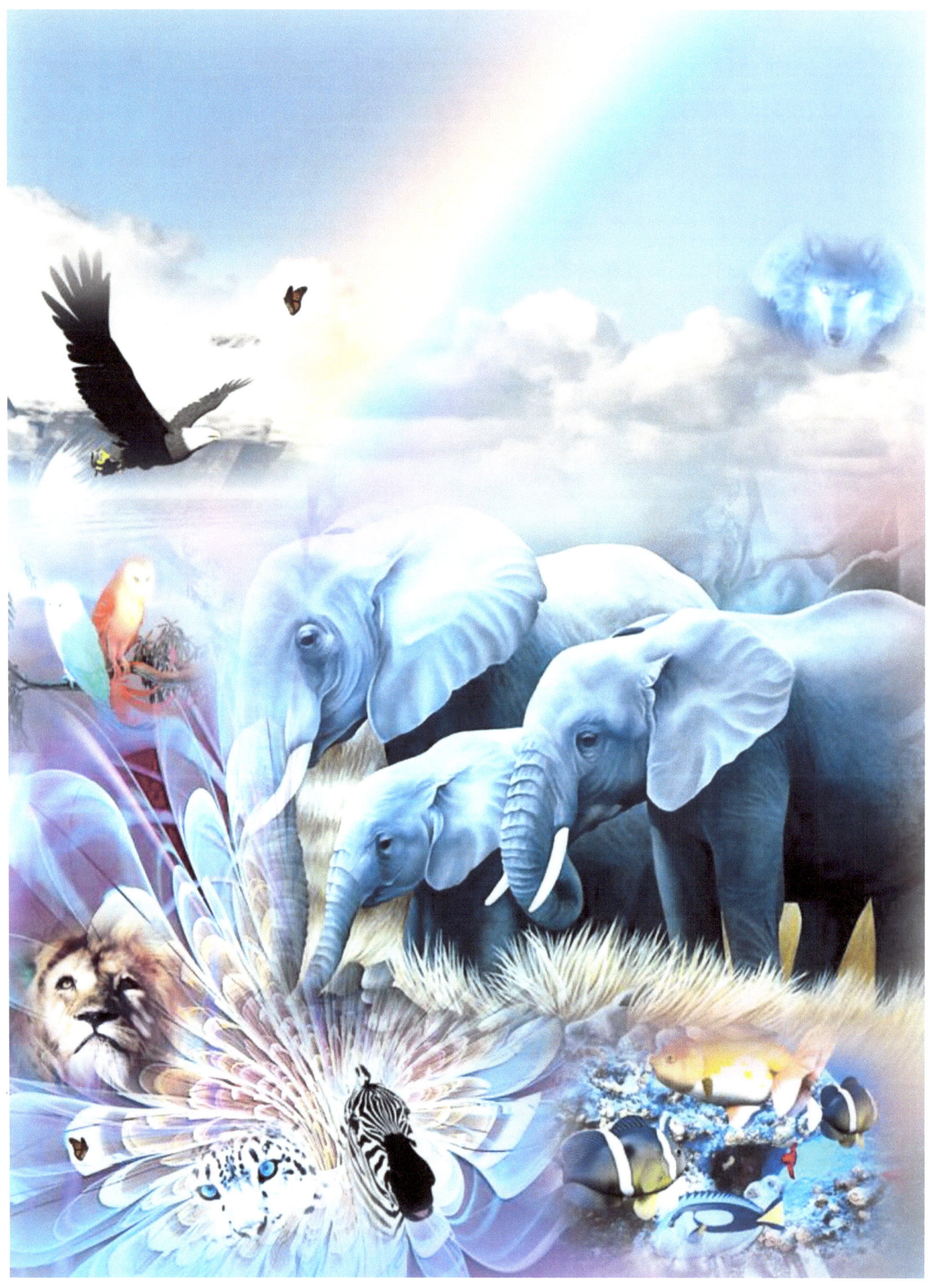

We need to save the animals, and ourselves..too.
We need to preserve the green, red, yellow and blue!
Save the innocence of this planet Earth.
For God gave us this responsibility of great worth..
To protect and preserve this Gift of His..

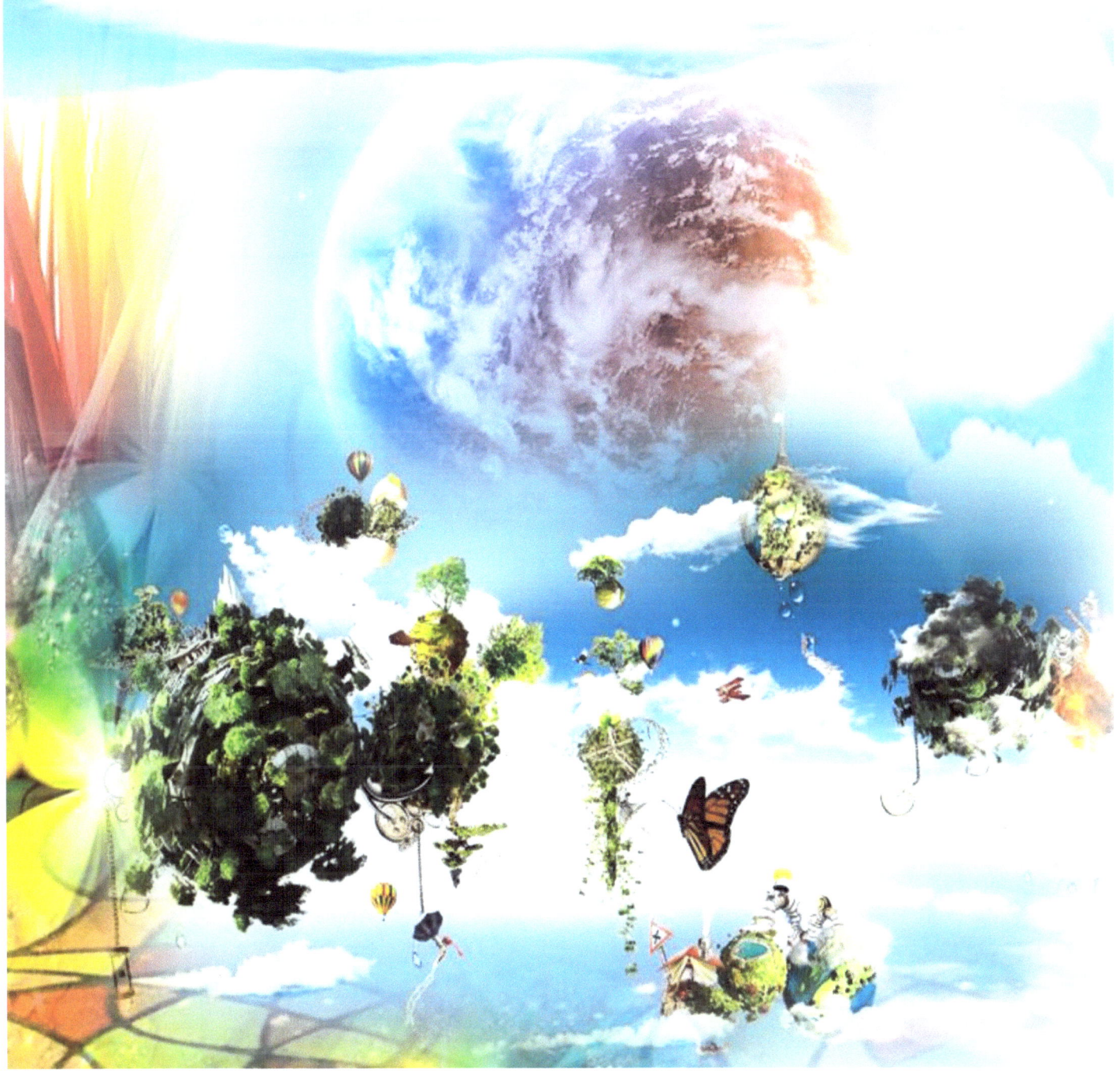

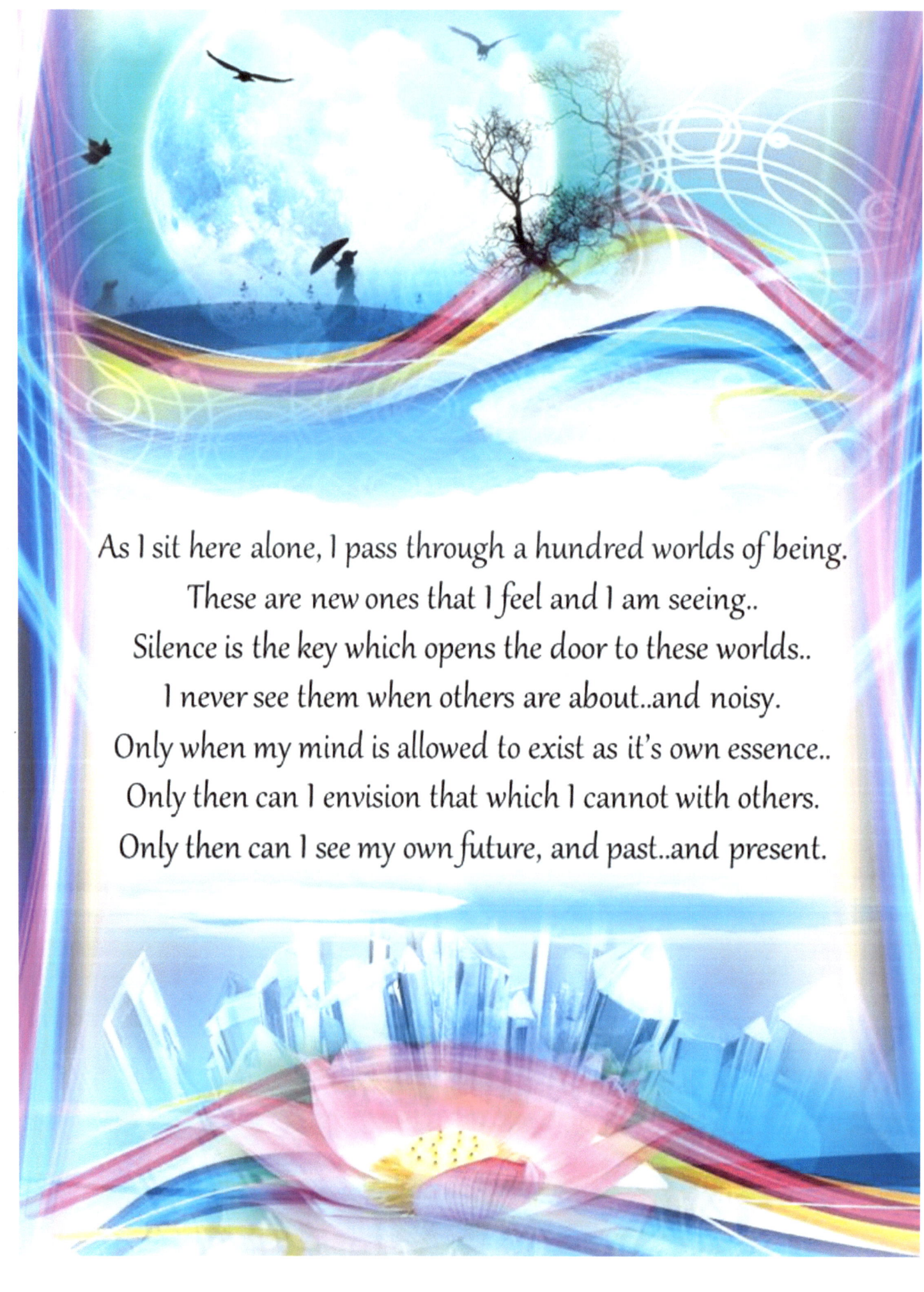

As I sit here alone, I pass through a hundred worlds of being.

These are new ones that I feel and I am seeing..

Silence is the key which opens the door to these worlds..

I never see them when others are about..and noisy.

Only when my mind is allowed to exist as it's own essence..

Only then can I envision that which I cannot with others.

Only then can I see my own future, and past..and present.

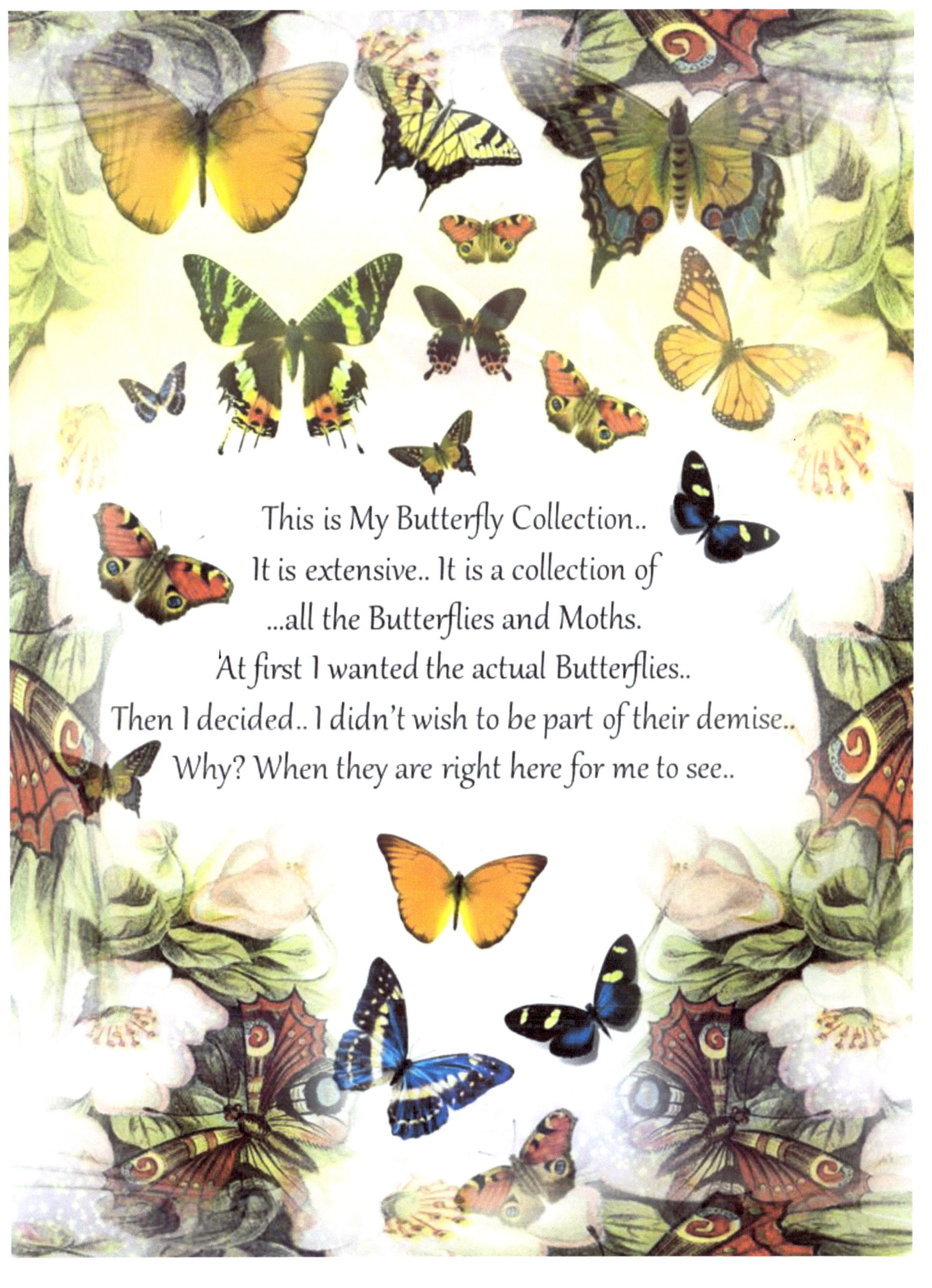

This is My Butterfly Collection..
It is extensive.. It is a collection of
...all the Butterflies and Moths.
At first I wanted the actual Butterflies..
Then I decided.. I didn't wish to be part of their demise..
Why? When they are right here for me to see..

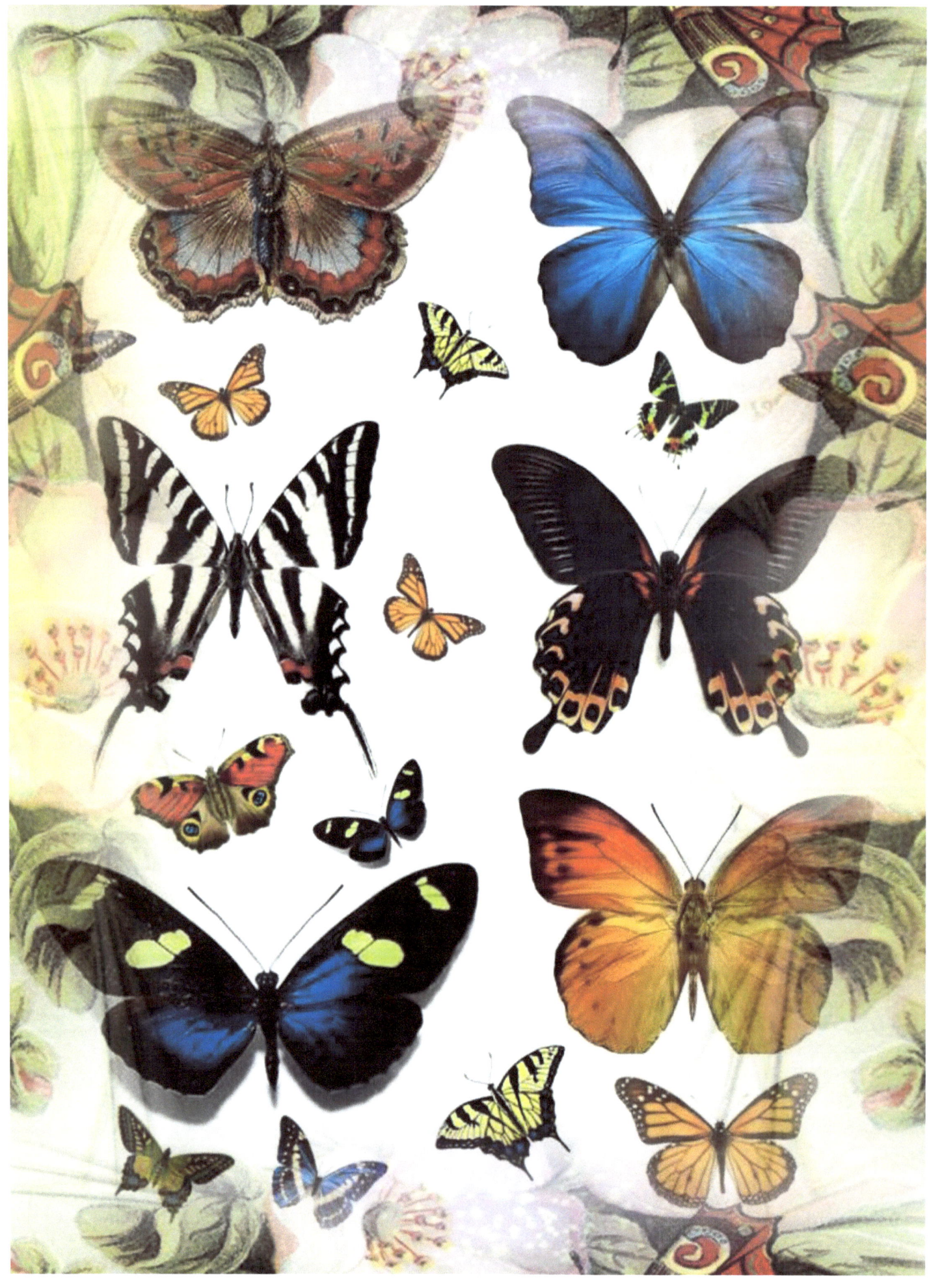

Time is running out for this planet Earth of ours..
Tick Tock ...Tick Tock..so go the hours..
Be Here Now...it's all we truly have to share...pilgrims!
The moment is yours..Carpe Diem, Robin Williams!

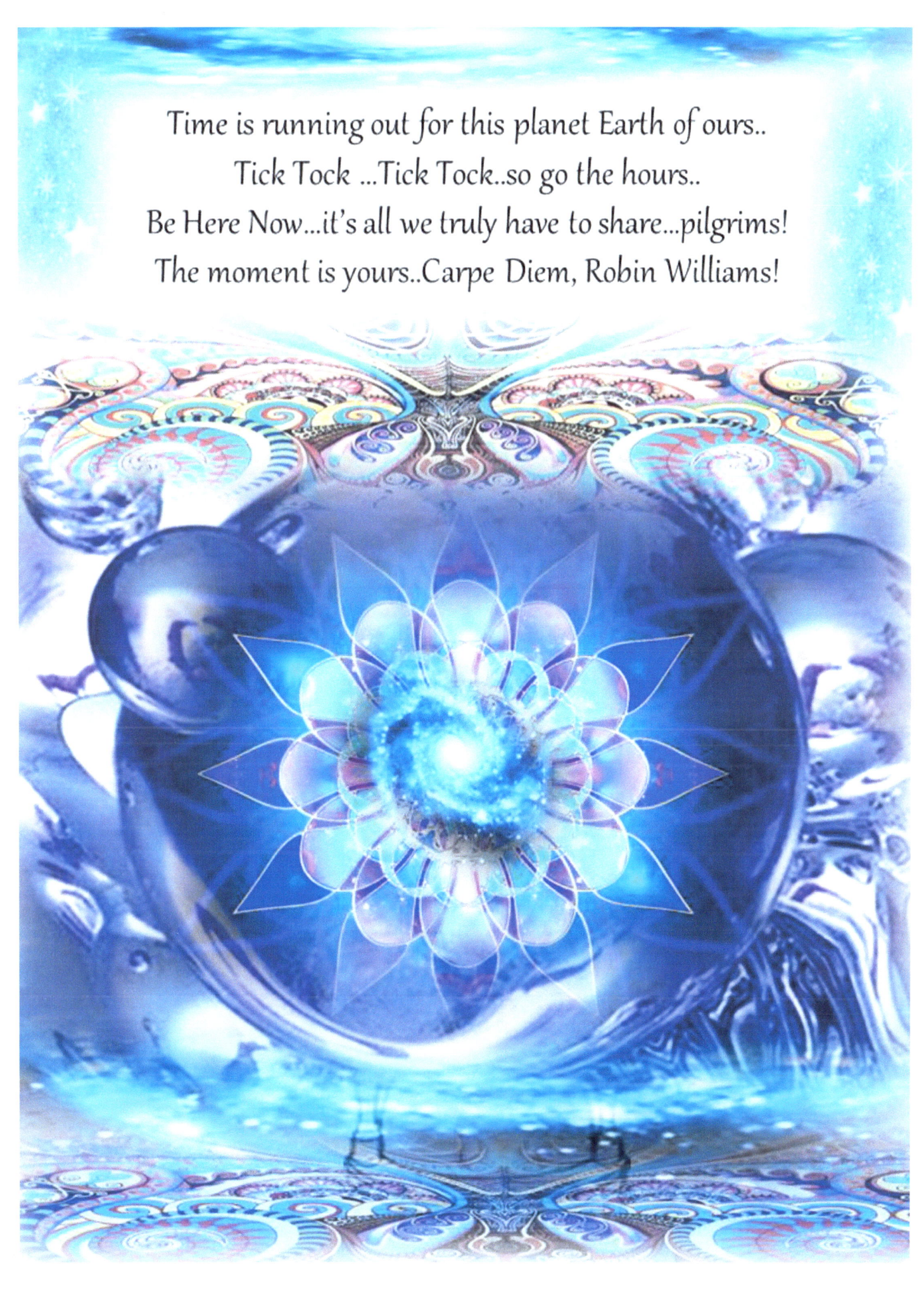

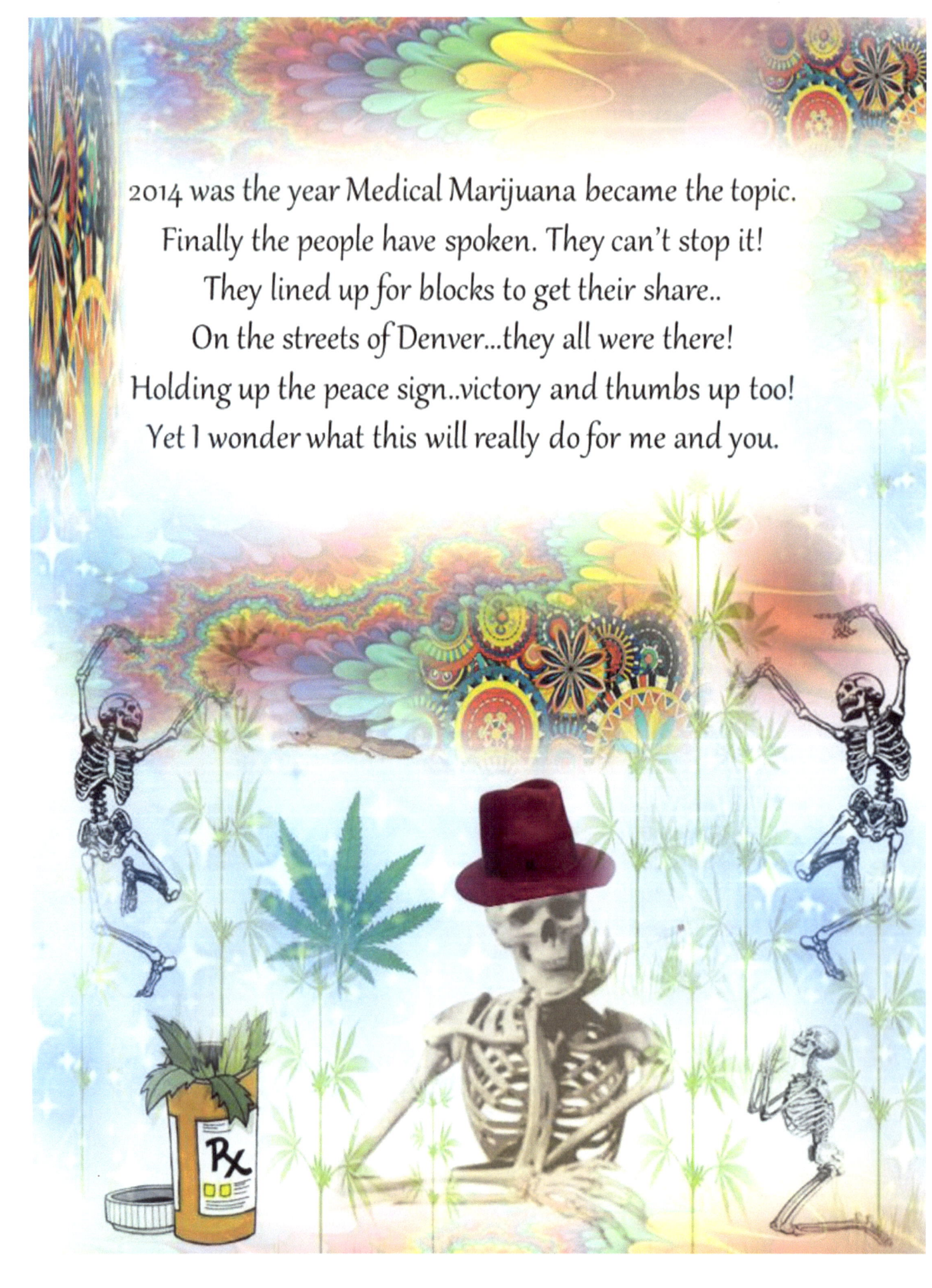

2014 was the year Medical Marijuana became the topic.
Finally the people have spoken. They can't stop it!
They lined up for blocks to get their share..
On the streets of Denver...they all were there!
Holding up the peace sign..victory and thumbs up too!
Yet I wonder what this will really do for me and you.

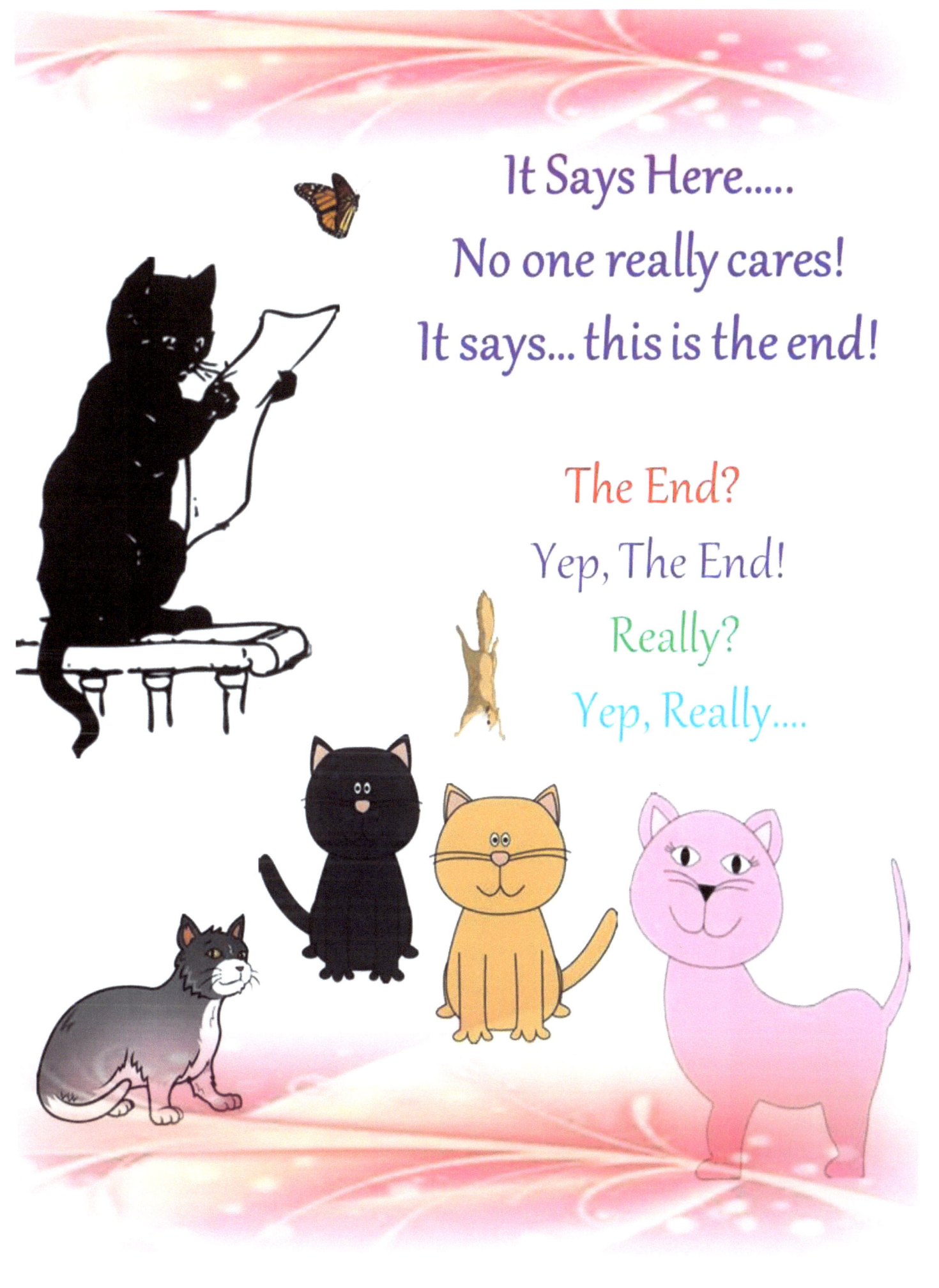

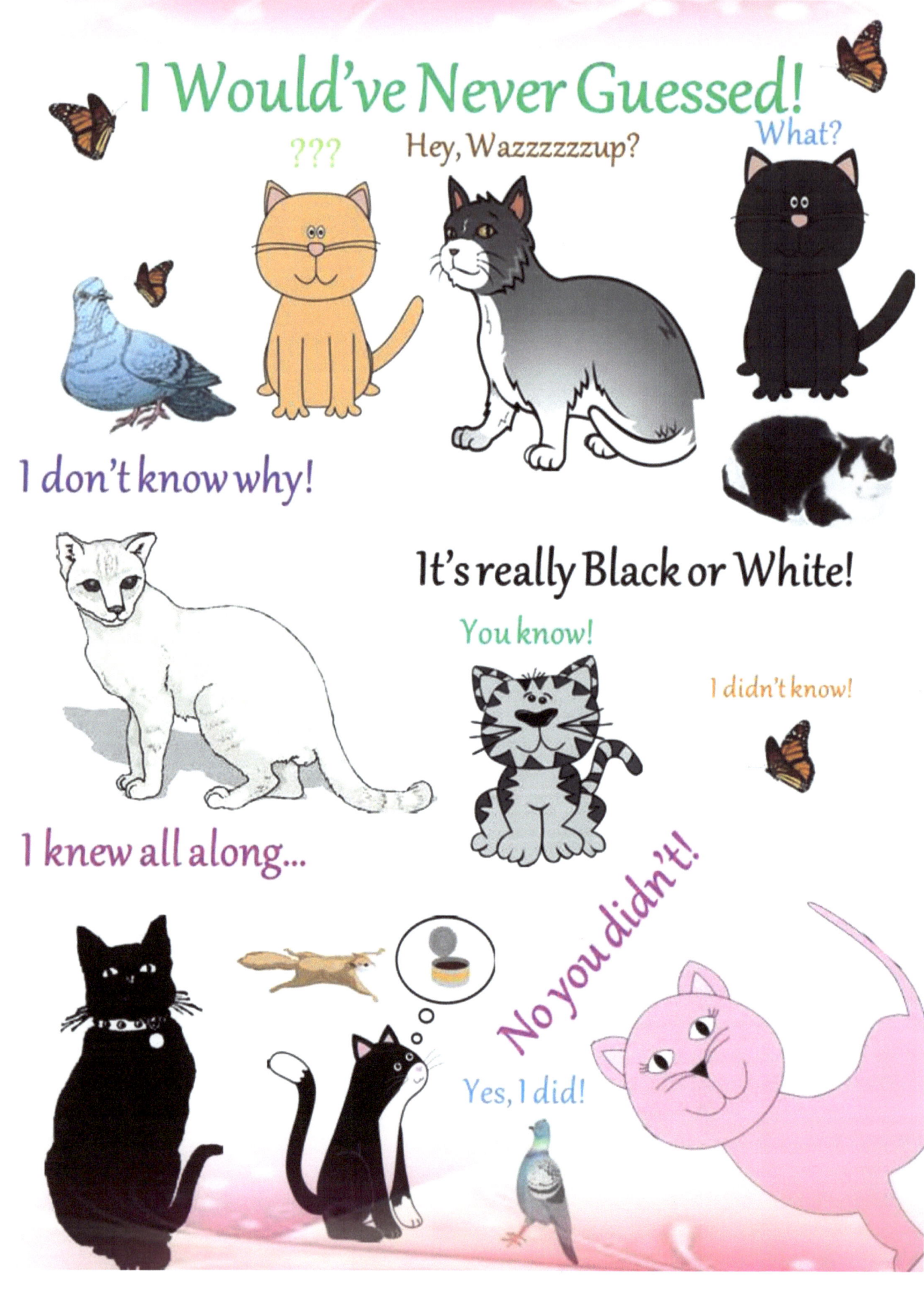

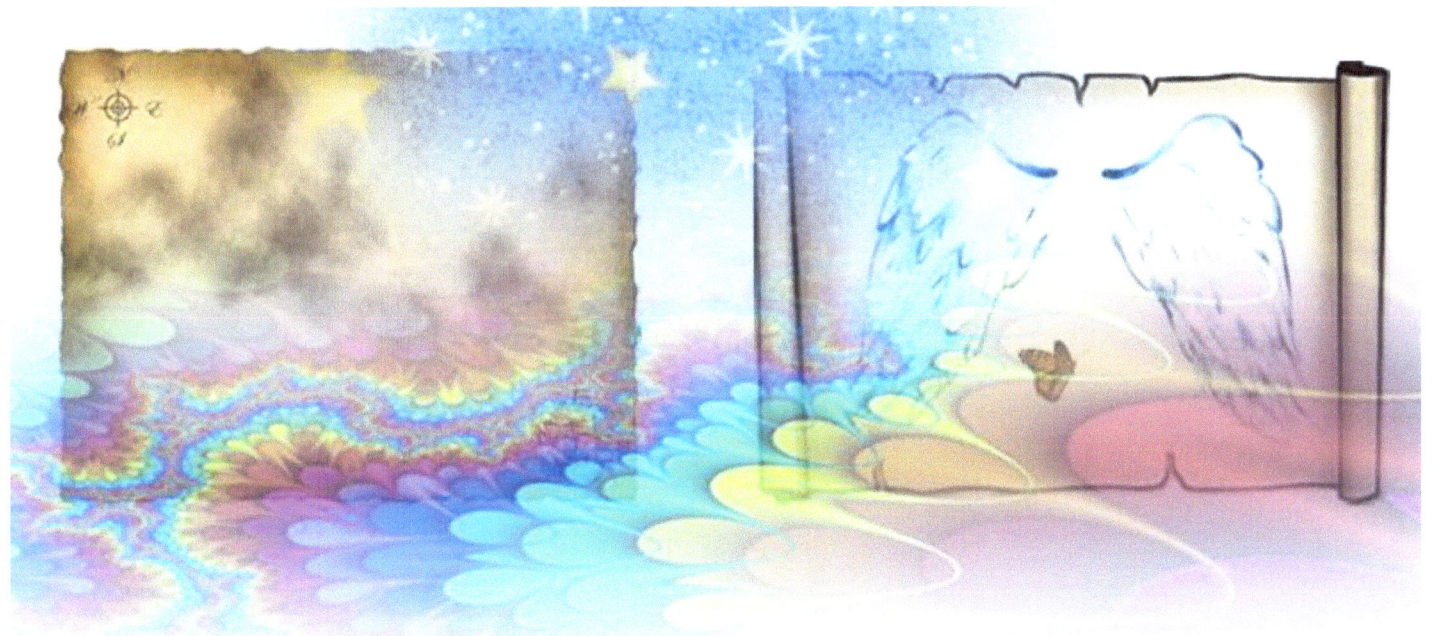

When people ask me for favors I thank them..
They just gave me a chance to earn a feather, a heavenly gem!
A feather for you..a feather for me.
'Cause this is how it works..you see!

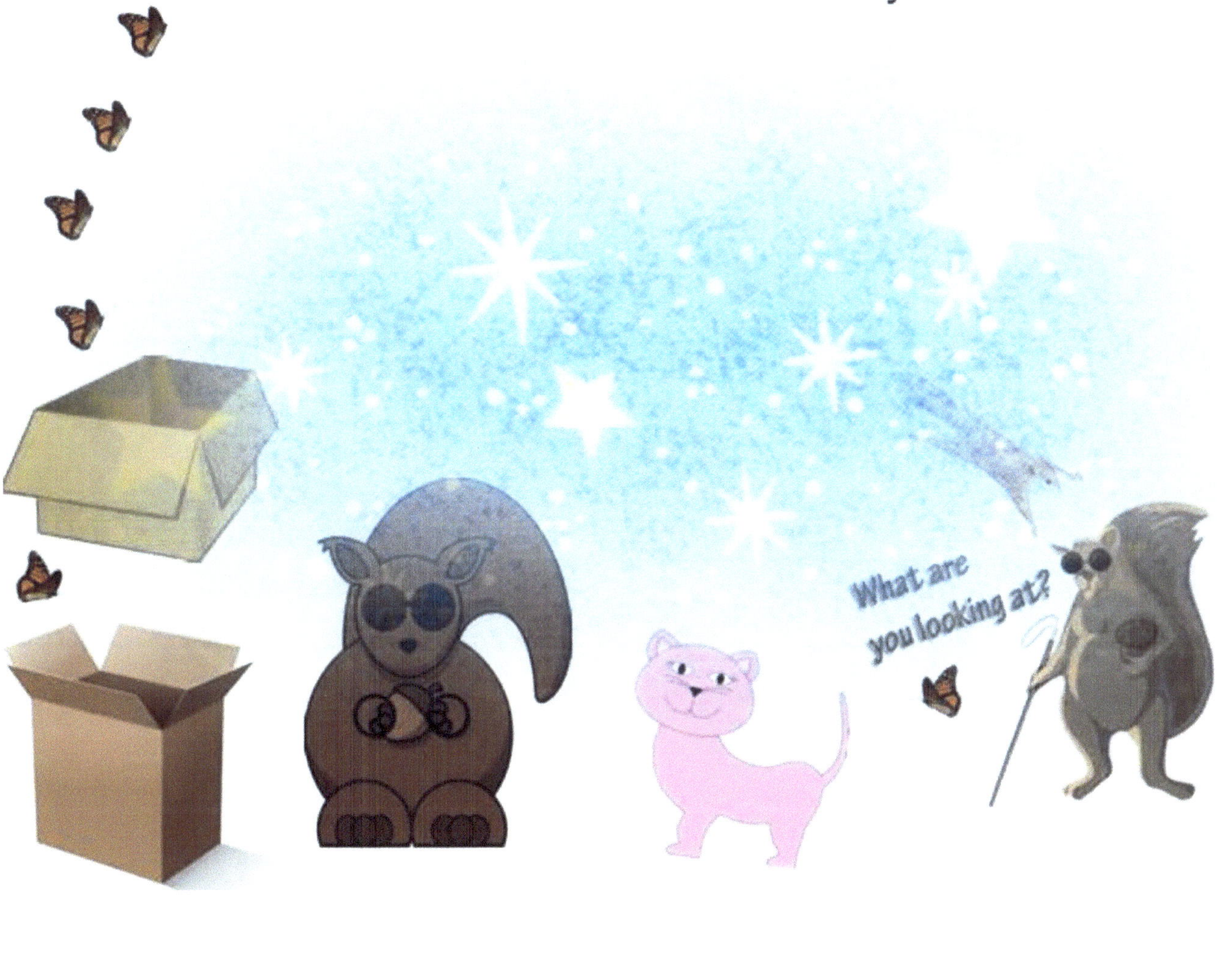

What are
you looking at?

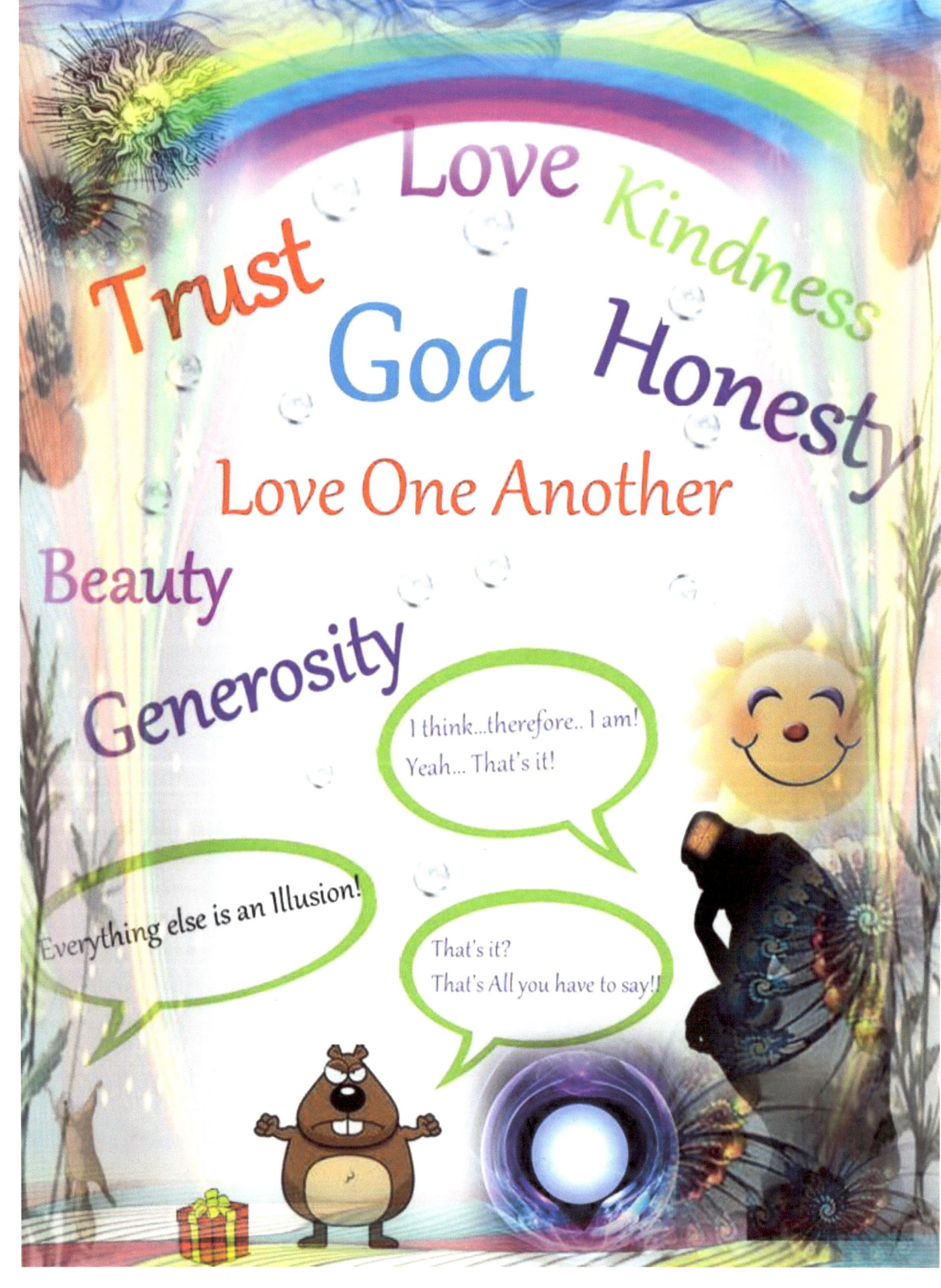

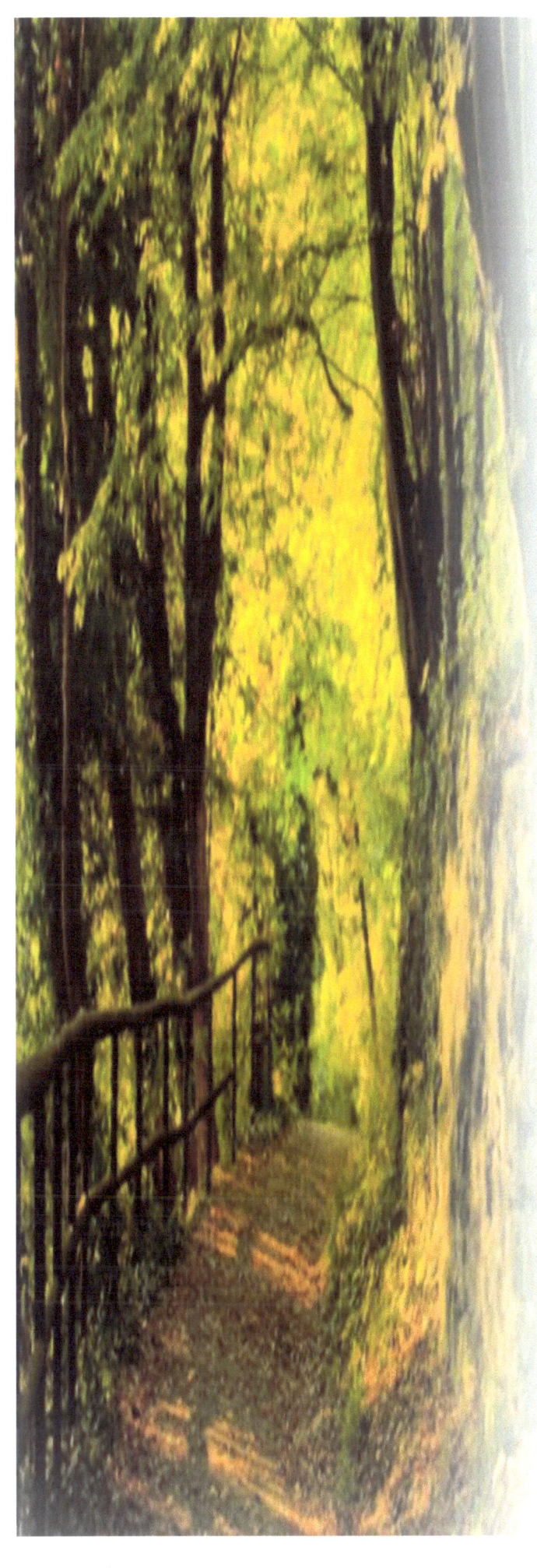

The Road Not Taken
By Robert Frost

Two roads diverged in a yellow wood,
And sorry I could not travel both
And be one traveler, long I stood
And looked down one as far as I could
To where it bent in the undergrowth;

Then took the other, as just as fair,
And having perhaps the better claim,
Because it was grassy and wanted wear;
Though as for that the passing there
Had worn them really about the same,

And both that morning equally lay
In leaves no step had trodden black.
Oh, I kept the first for another day!
Yet knowing how way leads on to way,
I doubted if I should ever come back.

I shall be telling this with a sigh
Somewhere ages and ages hence:
Two roads diverged in a wood, and I—
I took the one less traveled by,
And that has made all the difference.

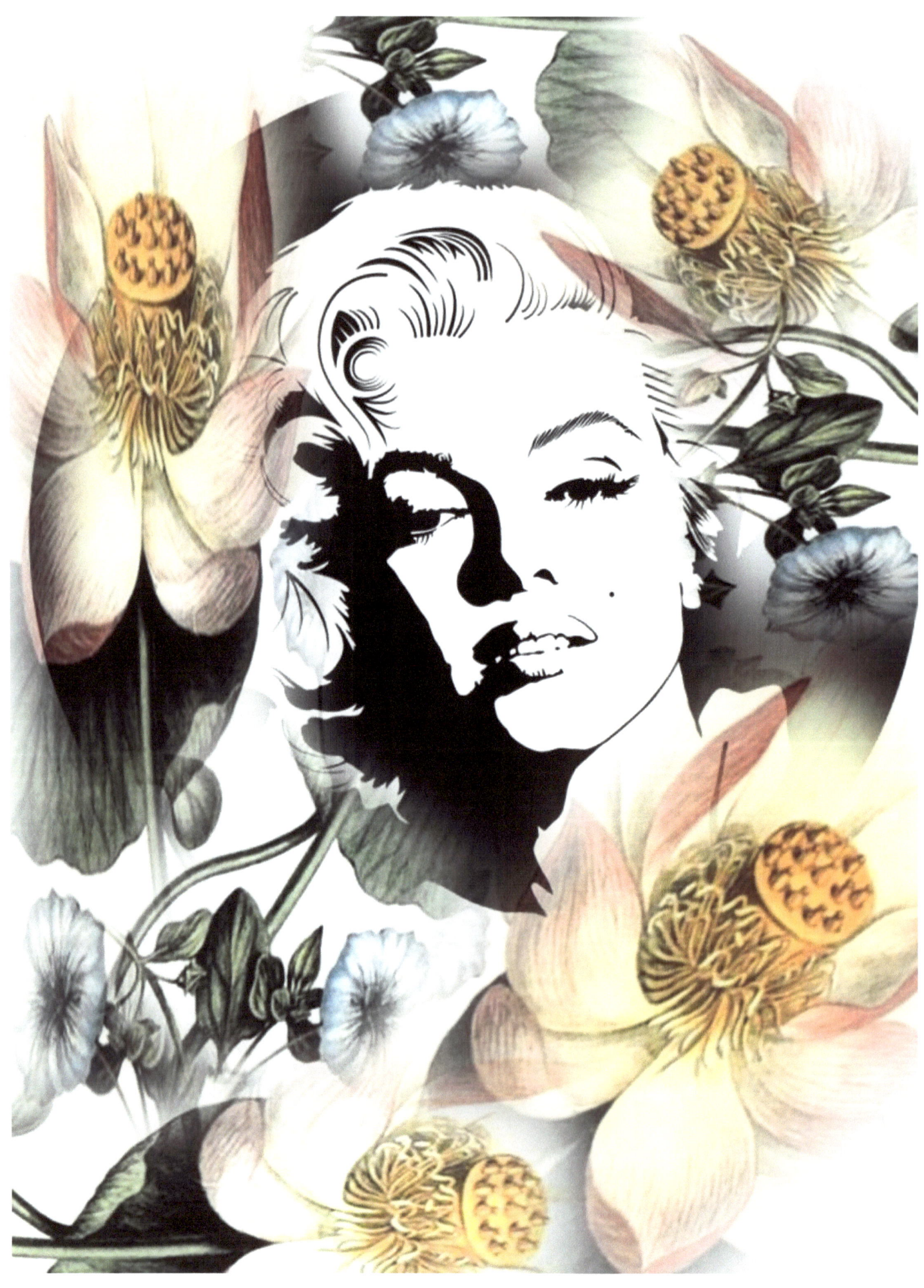

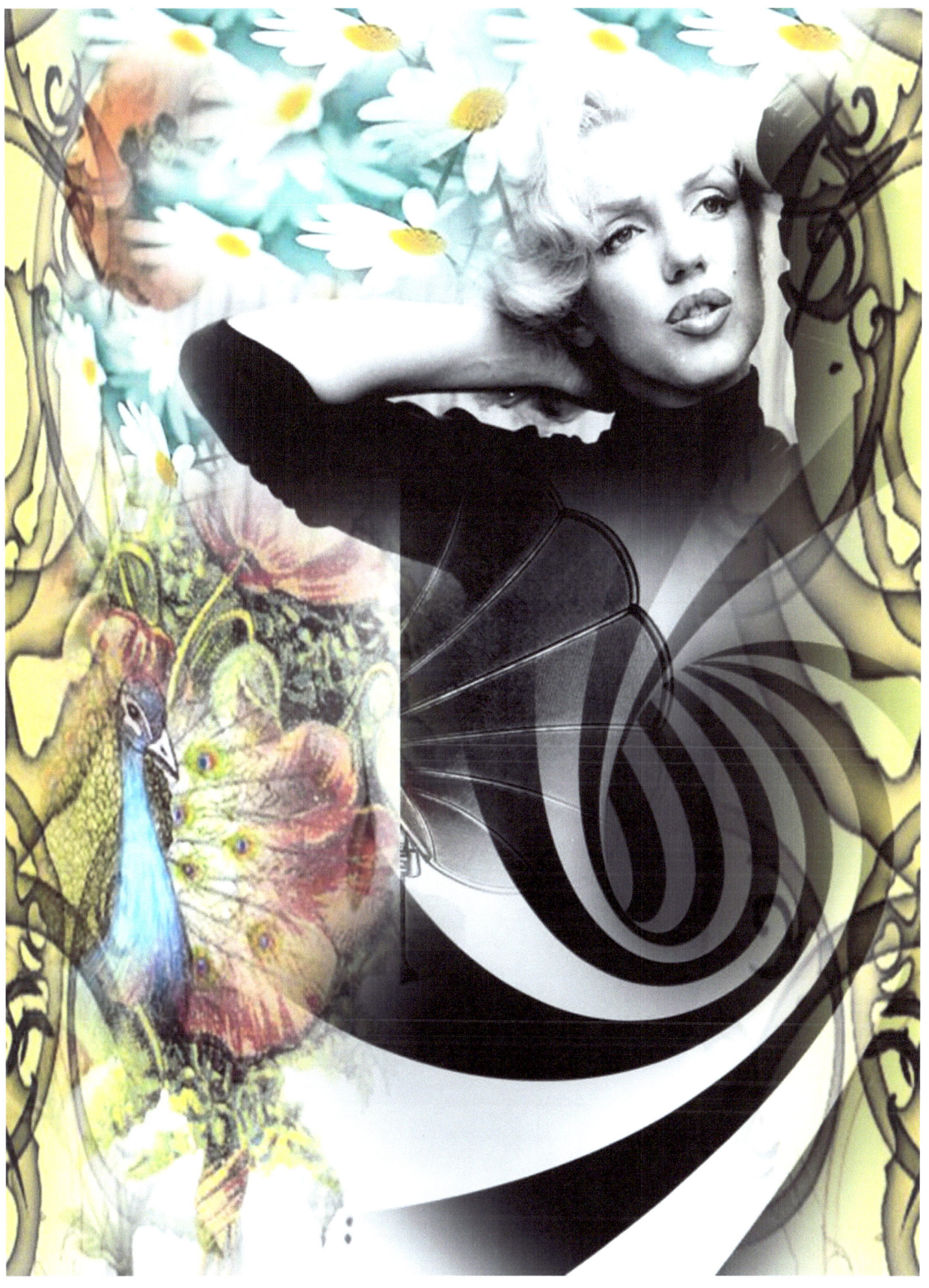

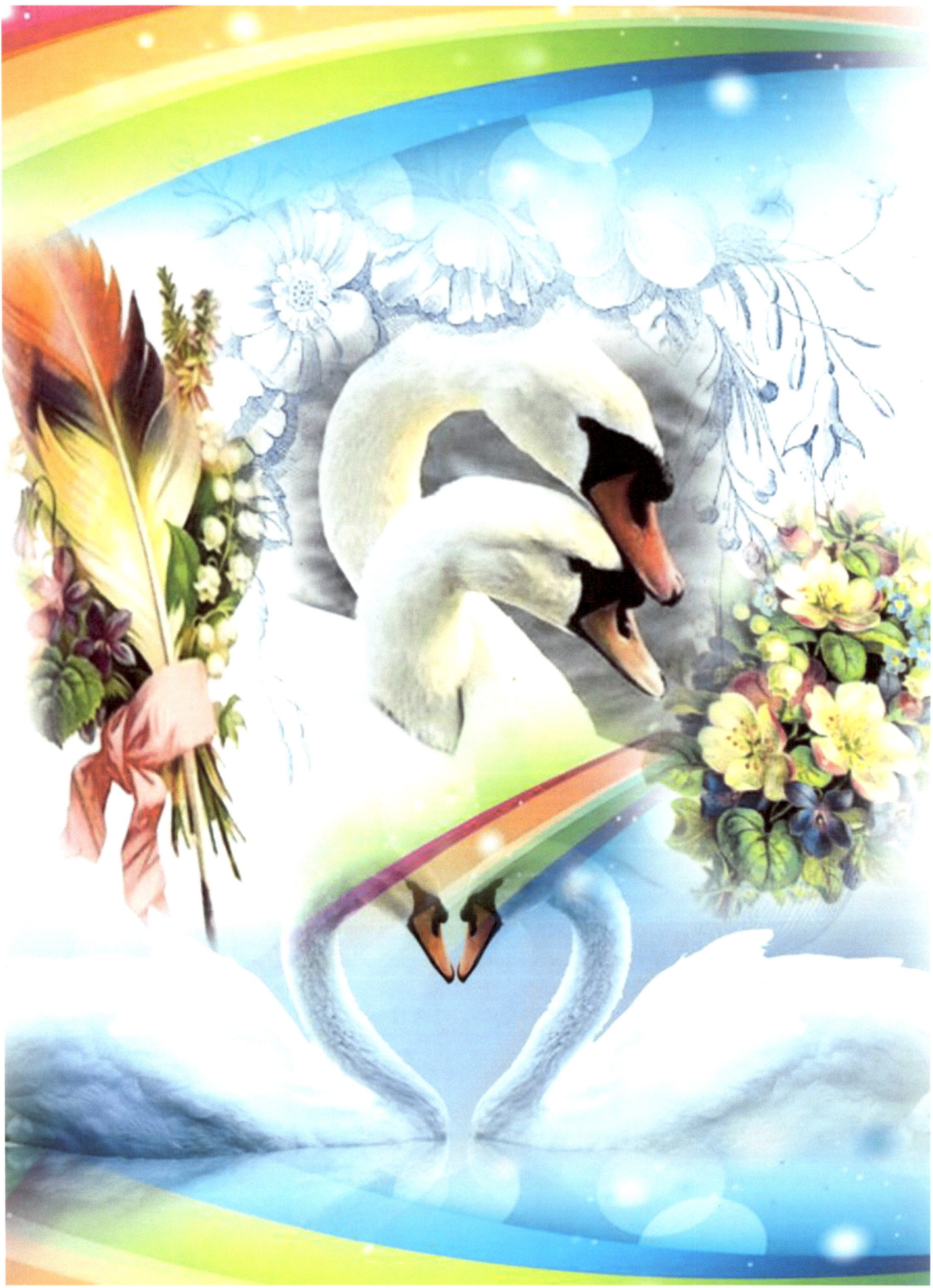

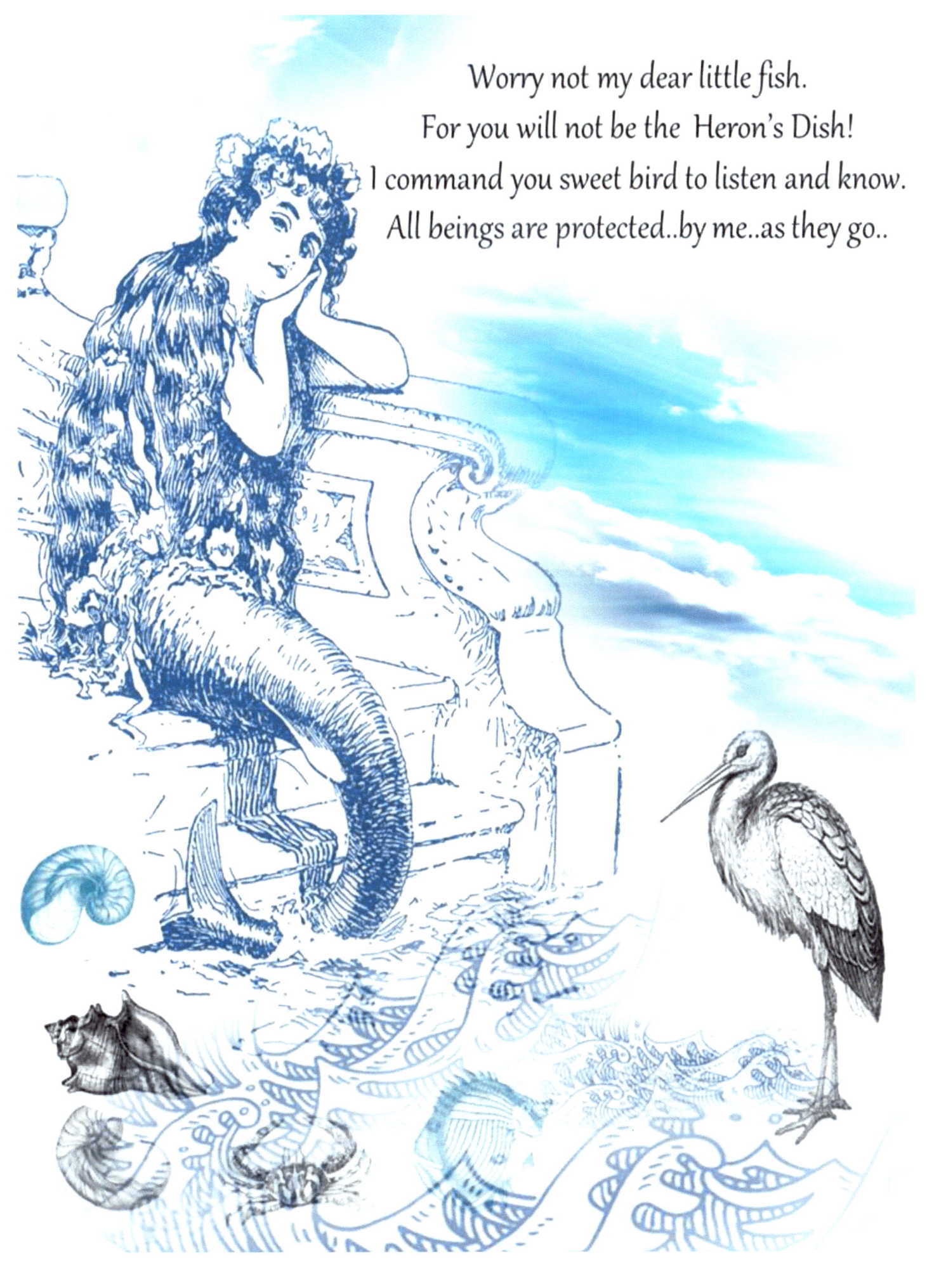

Worry not my dear little fish.
For you will not be the Heron's Dish!
I command you sweet bird to listen and know.
All beings are protected..by me..as they go..

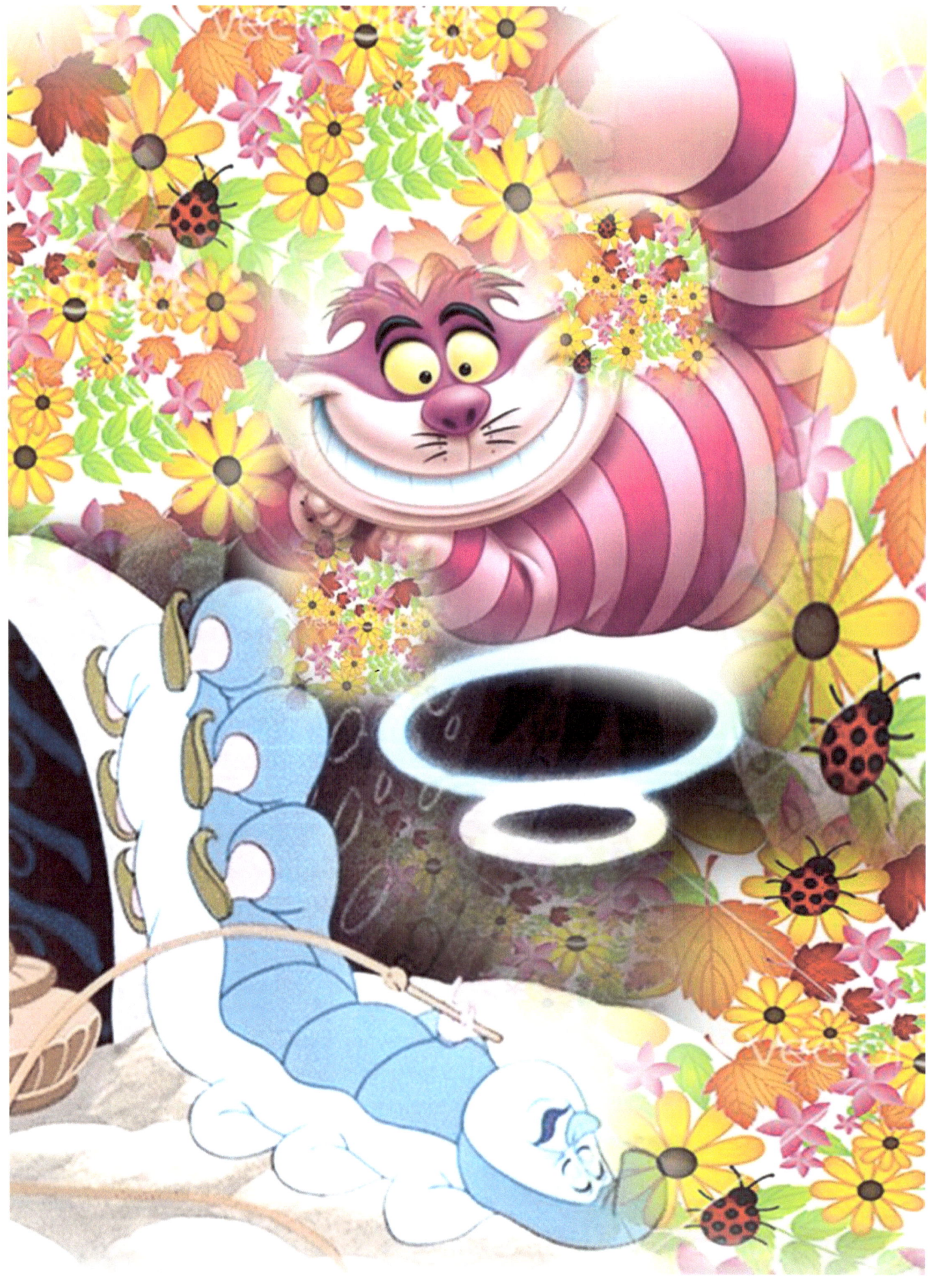

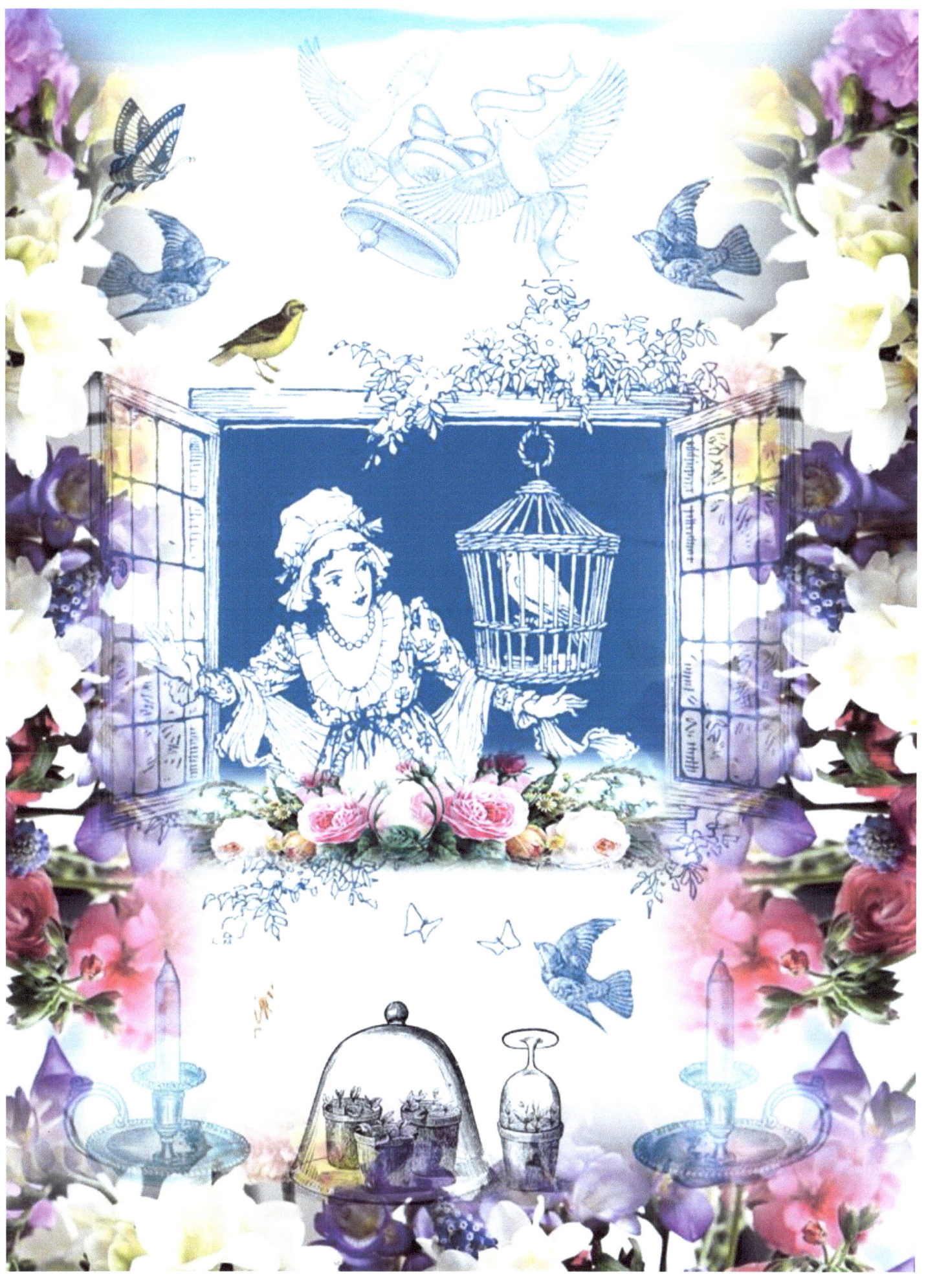

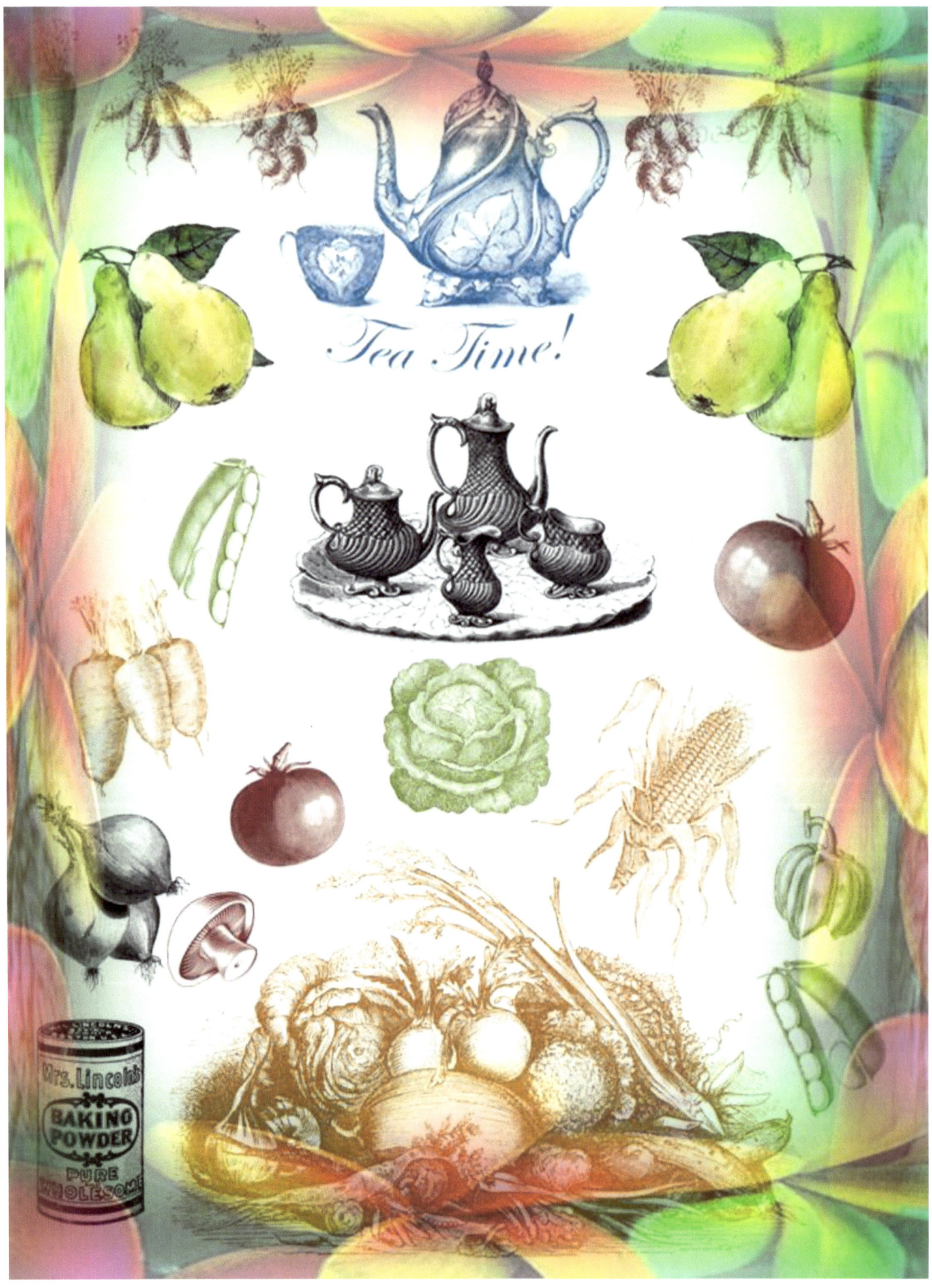

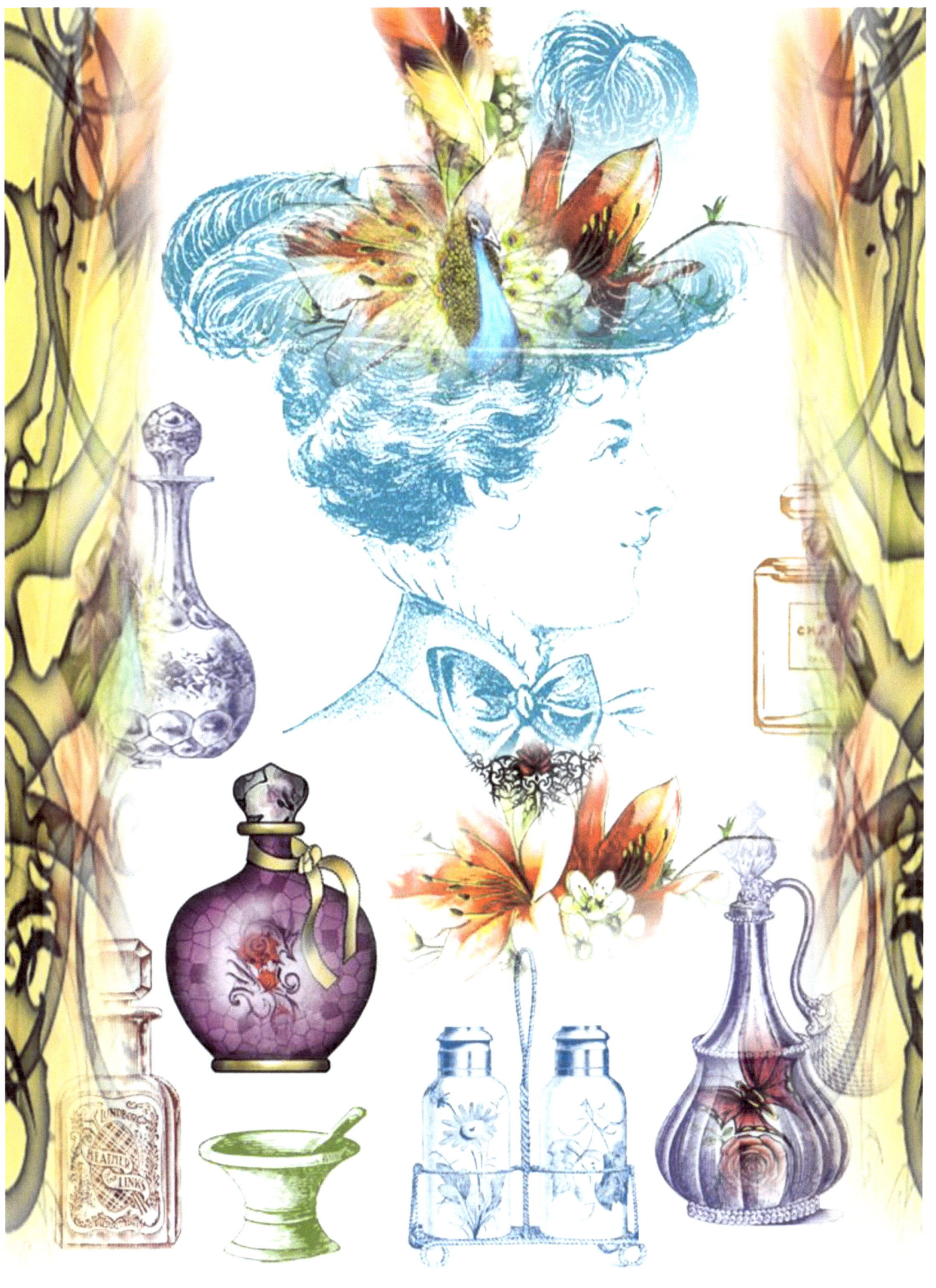

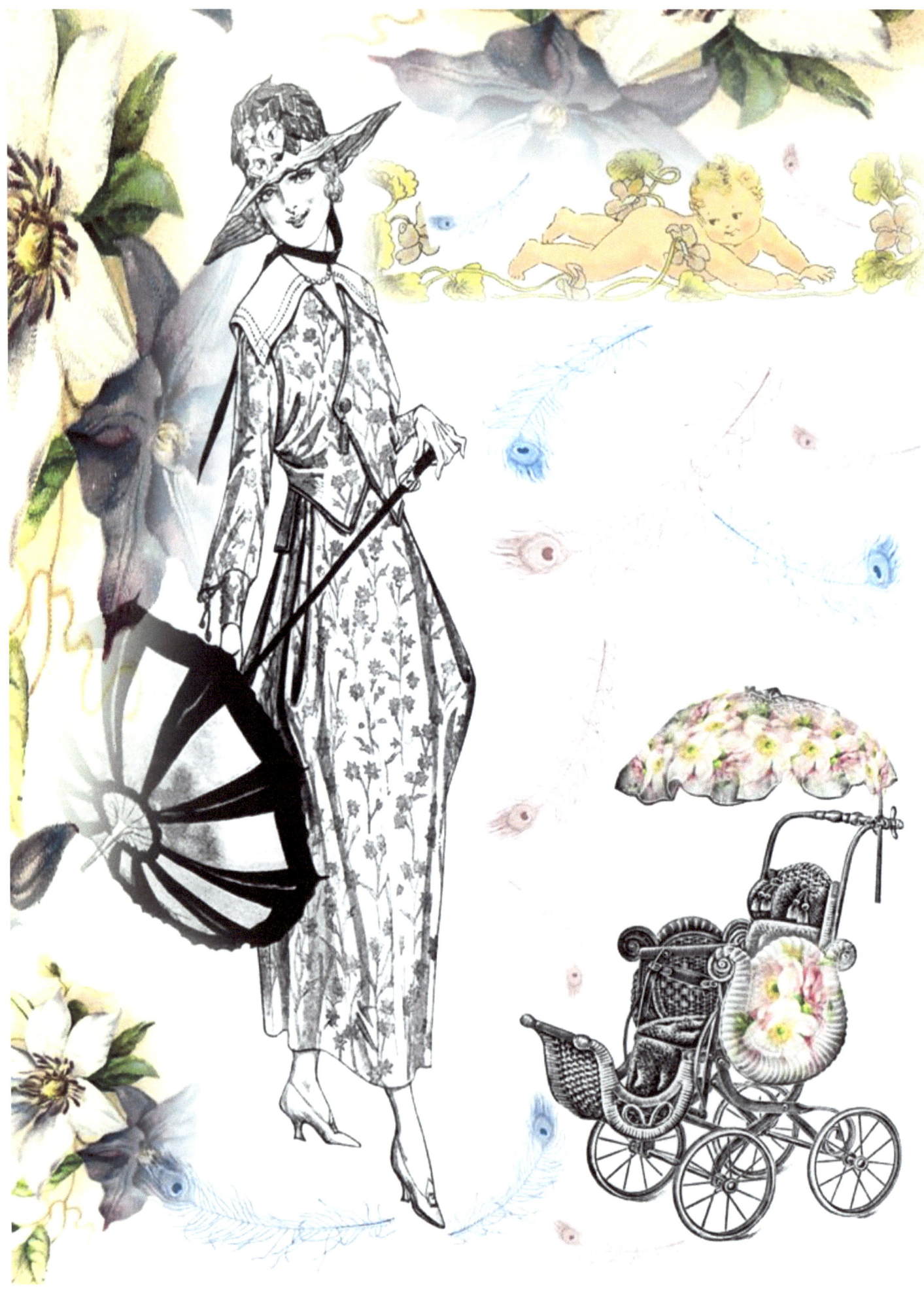

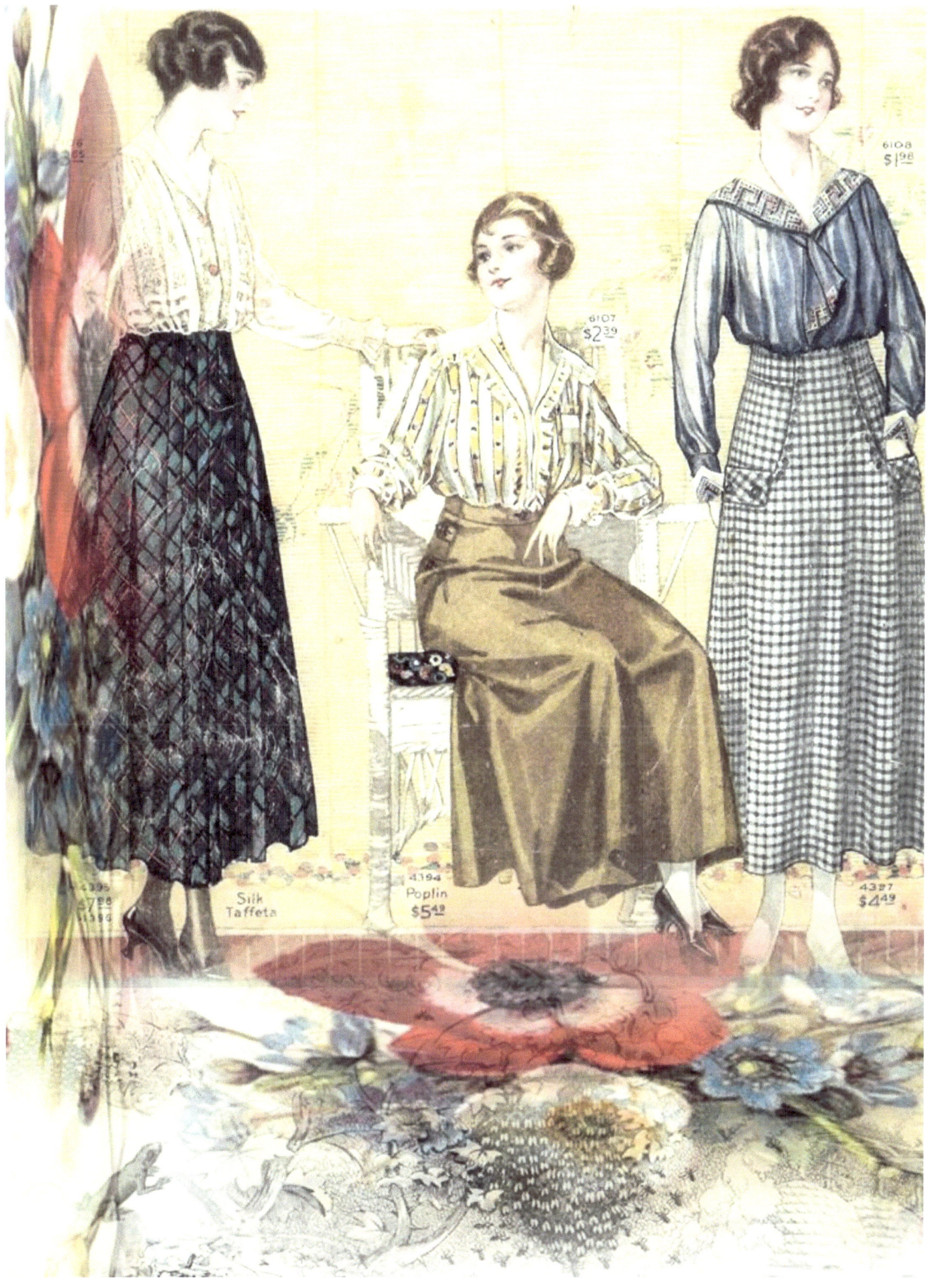

6108
$1.98

6107
$2.39

Silk
Taffeta

4194
Poplin
$5.49

4327
$4.49

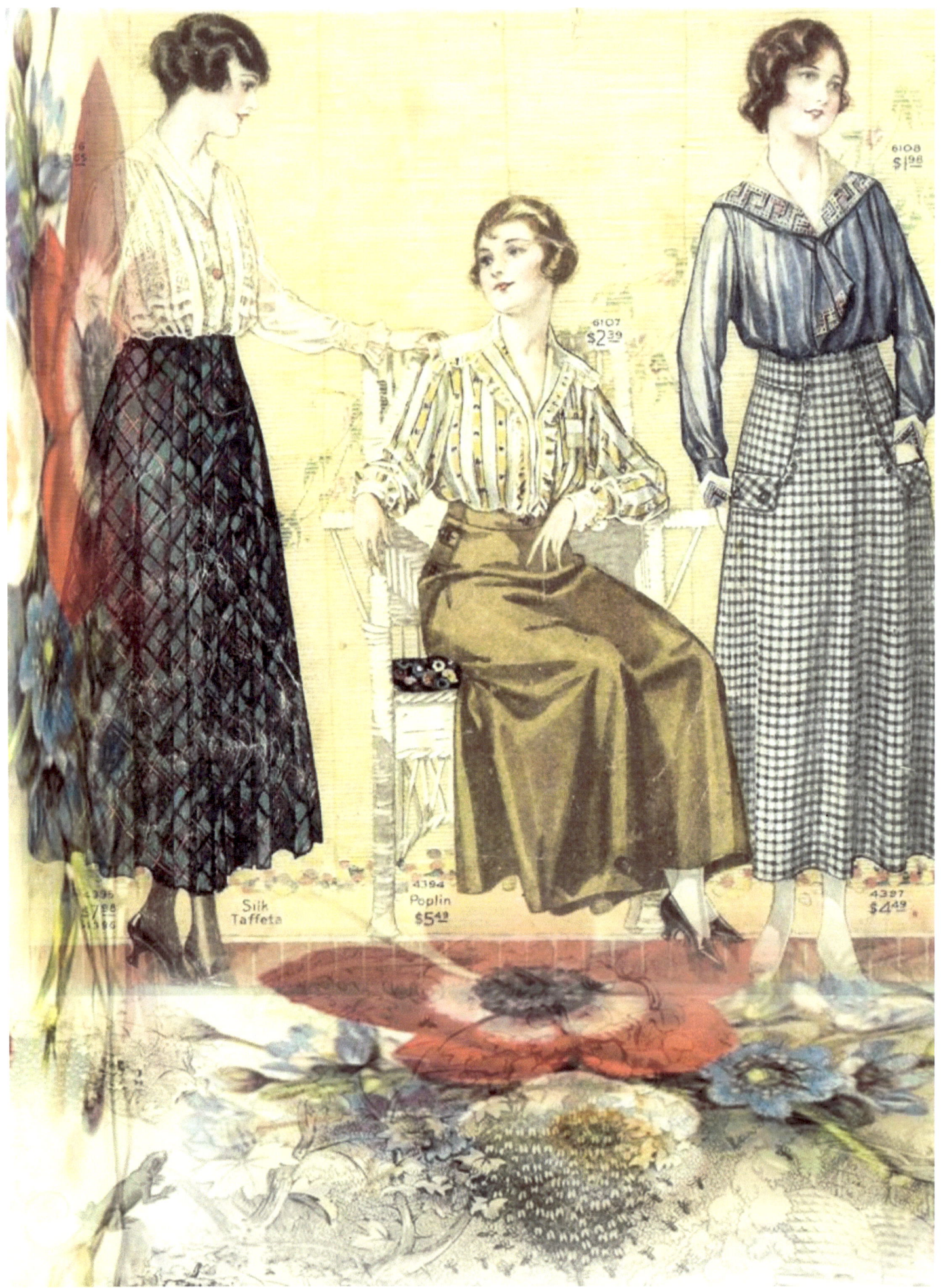

6108
$1.98

6107
$2.39

4395
4788
4396
Silk
Taffeta

4394
Poplin
$5.49

4397
$4.49

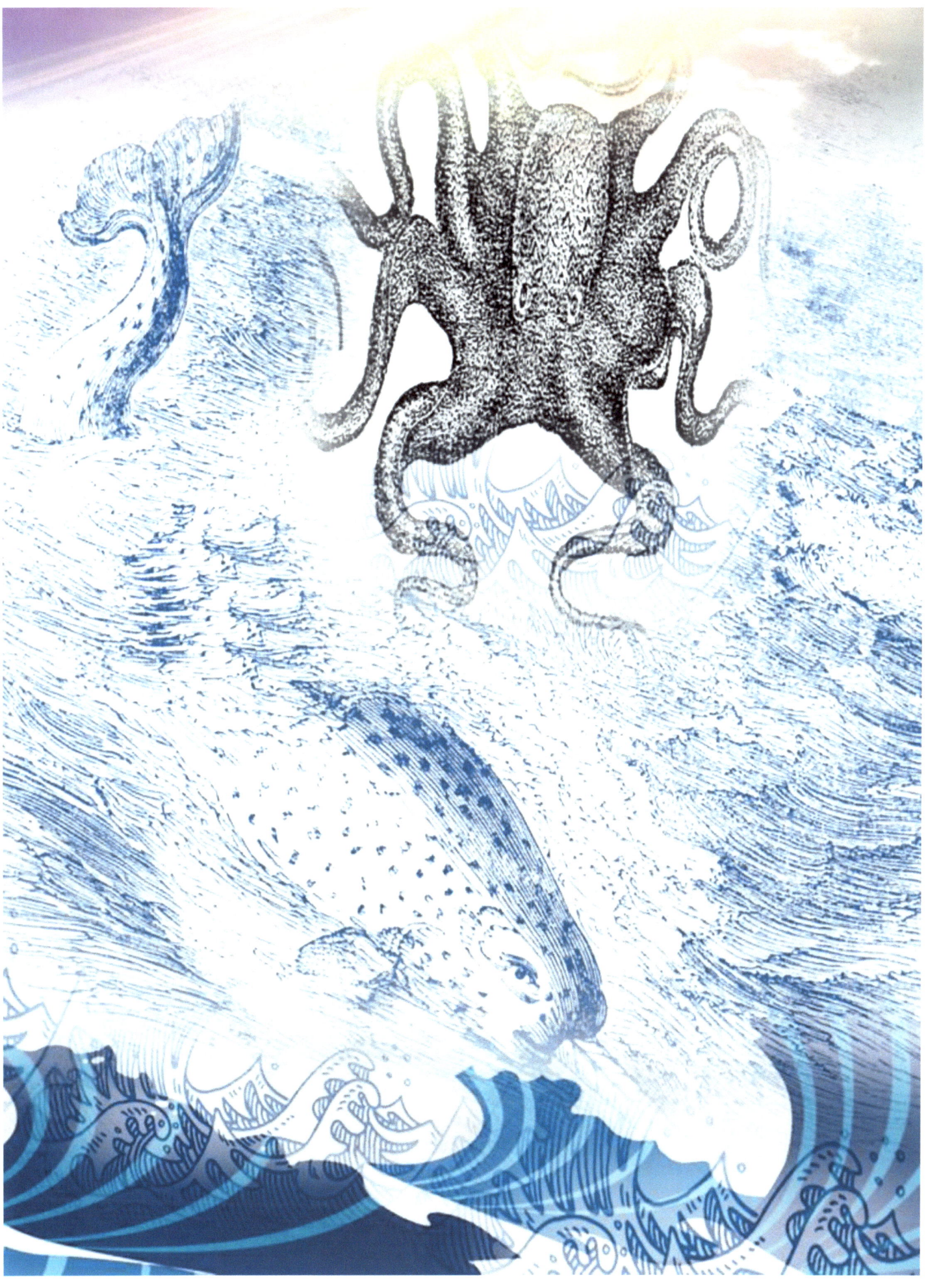

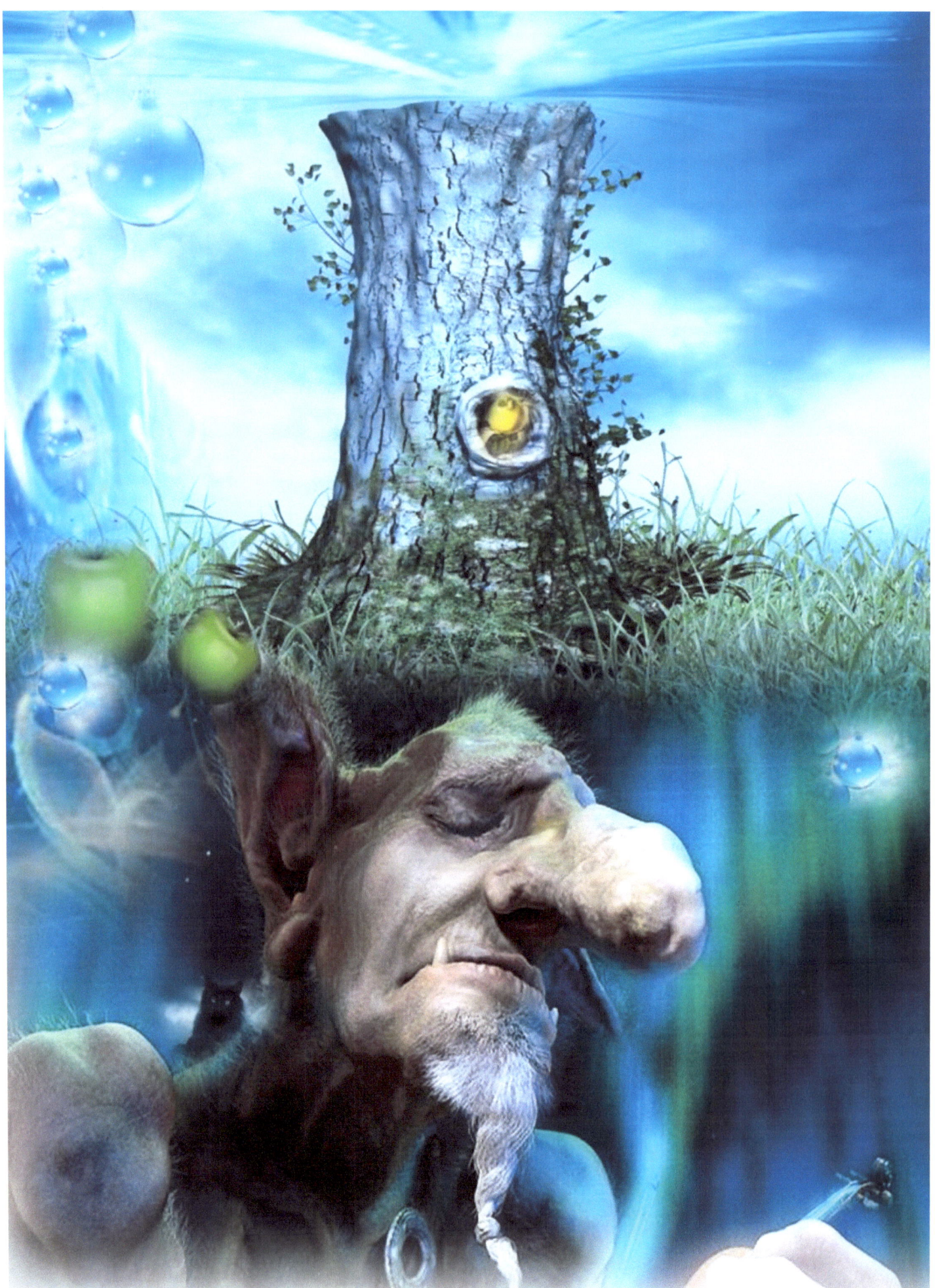

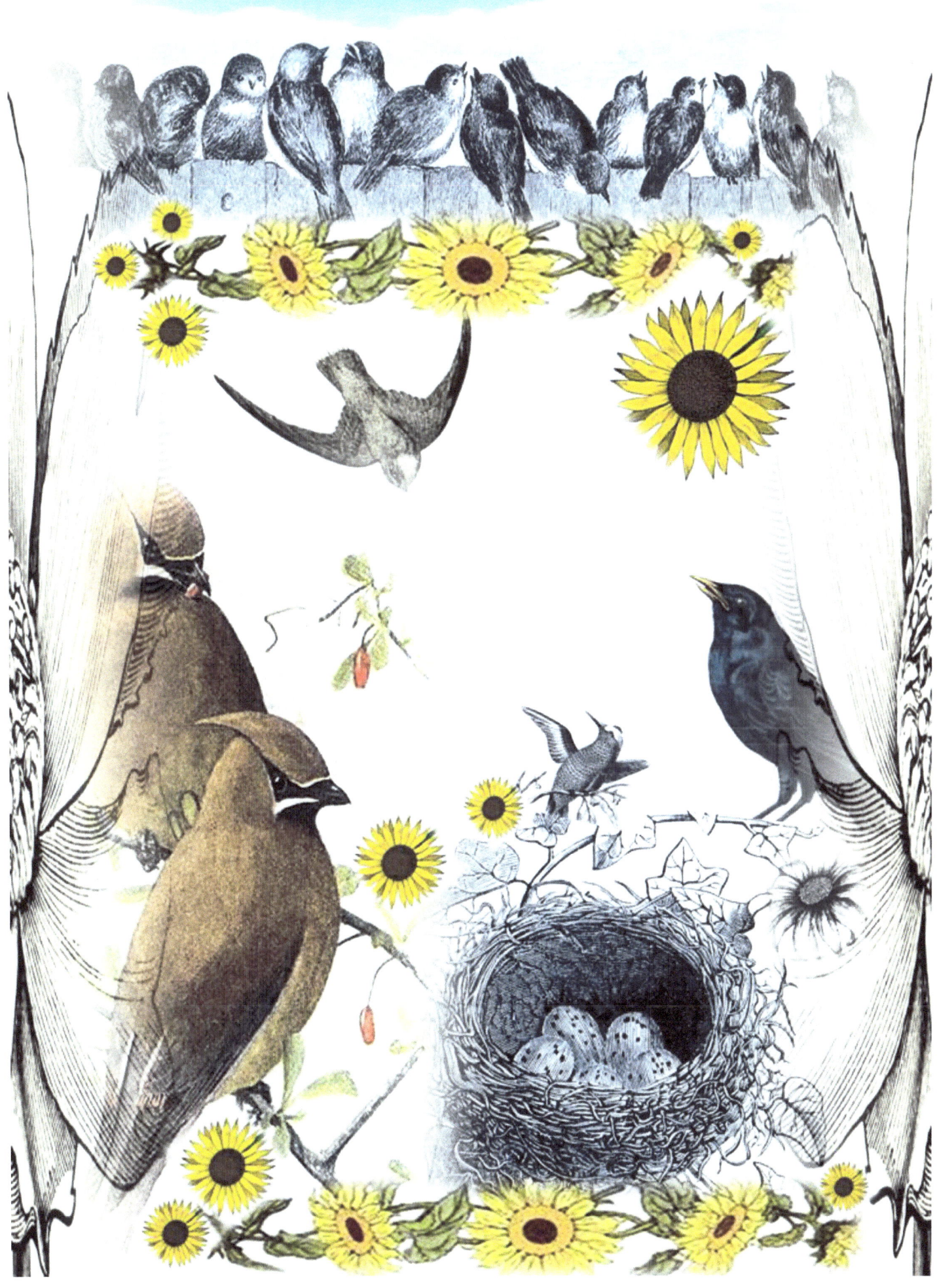

www.ingramcontent.com/pod-product-compliance
Lightning Source LLC
Chambersburg PA
CBHW050756180526
45159CB00003B/1486